RASHI

ON THE TORAH

פירוש רש"י על התורה

VOLUME 1

Selected portions of
Rashi on the Torah

Annotated and
Translated
by
Rabbi Avraham Yaakov Finkel

YESHIVATH BETH MOSHE
SCRANTON, PA.

CONTENTS

הקדמה

מראש הישיבה

מורינו הרב יעקב שניידמאן שליט״א

בילדותי שמעתי ששאל אחד מר׳ נפתלי מאמסטרדאם מתלמדי ר׳ ישראל מה לעשות אם יש לו ספקות באמונה. והשיב לו שילמד חומש ורש״י. ולמדנו מזה כחו של פירוש רש״י. ולכאו׳ פירוש רש״י אף שהוא הפירוש המובחר על החומש איזה מעלה מיוחדת יש לו בנוגע עניני אמונה. ומסברא היינו אומרים דהפירושים וספרים אחרים המסבירים עניני אמונה הם העקרים ליישר לב האדם באמונת הי״ת. וחידש ר׳ נפתלי דהספרים שמדברים בעניני אמונה אינם מיישרים לב האדם כפירוש רש״י על התורה.

וי״ל דשאר לימודים שבאו לפרש דרכים להשיג אמונת ה׳ אינם כמו פירוש רש״י דהוי בחינת אמונה פשוטה. והיינו אמונה בלי ספקות. וביאר החפץ חיים ענין אמונה פשוטה דהנה אף שמדין תורה ידעינן שבנו של אדם הוא בנו רק משום רוב בעילות הלך אחר הבעל מכ״מ אצל הבן בלא זה נקבע שהוא אביו ואין לו ספק כלל ורק מי שנסתפק הוא שצריך לדין רוב. ואמר החפץ חיים דכמו כן בענין האמונה בהקב״ה המאמין האמיתי מאמין בלי ספקות כלל וכמו האדם שאינו מסתפק באביו. ופירוש רש״י הוא חיזוק גדול לאמונה כזה, דבפירושו לא תמצא בירורים למה יהא מאמין אלא אמונת הי״ת הוא דבר פשוט עד מאד, וכל פירושו הוא לאחר הנחה זו.

ונראה לבאר טעם שני בדבר. דמבואר בש״ע הרב הל׳ תלמוד תורה הל׳ יב׳ ויג׳ דבתורה שבכתב אם מוציא בשפתיו אף על פי שאינו מבין אפילו פירוש המלות הרי זה מקיים מצות ולמדתם אבל בתורה שבע״פ אם אינו מבין הפירוש אינו נחשב לימוד כלל.

ולכאו׳ קשה למה יוצא מצות לימוד תורה אם אינו מבין כלל, דאע״פ שאמר המלות לכאו׳ אין לו קשר כלל עם המלות בלי הבנה.

ונראה דבתורה שבכתב מלבד הלימוד שיש בהבנת העניינים יש
קדושה במילות והאותיות. ועיין בהקדמת הרמב"ן על התורה, וז"ל
עוד יש בידינו קבלה של אמת כי כל התורה כולה שמותיו של הקב"ה
שהתיבות מתחלקות לשמות בעניין אחד עכ"ל ונמצא דמלבד הבנת
העניינים, כל התורה כולה הוא שמות של הקב"ה, וכל כח בעולם יש
לו שורש בשמות הללו. ונראה דזהו הטעם דהלומד תורה שבכתב
ואינו מבין כלל קיים המצוה דהרי מוציא בפיו שמות של הקב"ה,
ואמירתו מוציא מוציא כח הקדושה שיש בכל שם.

ונראה דפירוש רש"י על התורה יש בו גם מעין מעלה זו ואף
דודאי עיקרו הוא תורה שבע"פ ולא מקיים בו מצות תלמוד תורה אלא
על ידי שמבין מה שלומד מכ"מ יש בו עוד מעין מעלת תורה שבכתב
שפירושו הוא כמו לבוש של תורה שבכתב וע"י לימודו הוי כאילו
הוציא המילים של התורה הקדושה ונשפע עליו קדושת אותיות
התורה. ושמא אף מטעם זה אמר הרב נפתלי זצ"ל דלימוד תורה עם
פירוש רש"י פועל עליו חיזוק אמונה. הרחמן יזכנו למדרגת הקדושה
ששייך מלימוד רש"י על התורה.

SUMMARY OF
RABBI YAAKOV SCHNAIDMAN'S
PROLOGUE

———⊰◈⊱———

Rabbi Naftoli Amsterdam, a student of Rabbi Yisrael Salanter, was asked, "If one has doubts about his faith, what can he do to help himself?" Rabbi Naftoli Amsterdam responded that he should learn Rashi's commentary on the Torah.

Though one might think a person would gain more regarding matters of faith if he studied works that address concepts of faith directly, Rav Naftoli advises that philosophical works will not straighten out one's heart with the efficacy that the study of Rashi, the primary commentary on the Torah, will.

Possibly, this is because Rashi's commentary is based on simple faith, also known as faith without doubts. The Chofetz Chaim explained the concept of simple faith as follows. By Torah law we ascertain that one's father is indeed his father by adhering to the concept of following the majority. Since most children are conceived from the husband of their mother, we assume each child's father to be the mother's husband. However a biological son knows whom his father is and does not have to rely on the rule of following the majority. Likewise, ultimate faith in the Almighty is the faith of one who has no doubts. Rashi's commentary strengthens this type of

---

Rabbi Yaakov Schnaidman is the Rosh Yeshivah of Yeshivath Beth Moshe Scranton, Pennsylvania.

faith, because it does not contain philosophical proofs of faith; rather it is based on the preconceived acceptance of faith.

Another possible explanation is as follows: The Shulchan Aruch HaRav says that one fulfils the mitzvah of Torah study by reading the written text of the Torah, even if he does not understand what he is saying. (However the same is not true of the Oral Torah; if one does not understand what he is saying while learning the Oral Torah he does not fulfill the mitzvah.) One who does not understand what he is reading has no connection to the words, so how is it possible for him to fulfill the mitzvah of Torah study if he reads the written text without understanding what he is saying?

In his introduction to his commentary on the Torah, the Ramban writes that we have a tradition that the entire Written Torah is made up of Names of the Almighty; the sentences and words can be read in ways that reveal these Names, which are the source for everything that exists in the world. One who says the words of the Written Torah even without understanding them, connects to the holiness of the Names of Hashem contained in them thereby bringing holiness into this world.

Rashi's commentary also has this benefit, for when one understands the words of Rashi he fulfills the mitzvah of learning the Oral Torah, and since Rashi's words explain the Written Torah, it is as if he were saying the words of the Written Torah. Thus he becomes infused with the holiness of those words, thereby strengthening his faith as Rabbi Naftoli said.

May the Merciful One grant us the merit to attain the holiness inherent in Rashi's commentary on the Torah.

TRANSLATOR'S INTRODUCTION

———◈———

This volume contains insights from Rashi's commentaries on *sefer Bereishis* and *sefer Shemos*. Sparkling with timeless Torah thoughts, these gems of wisdom have been a source of inspiration and solace throughout the ages.

Rashi's commentary on the Torah is unparalleled; it has become a part of Jewish life. His words are studied daily by beginning students and advanced scholars alike, in the yeshivah and in the home. "Learning Chumash with Rashi" has become a familiar byword. In a concise yet lucid style Rashi explains the *p'shat*—the plain meaning of the text; defines unfamiliar words, often translating them into Old French; and frequently adds midrashic insights to illustrate a point. As he puts it: "I have come only [to teach] the plain meaning of the verse and the Aggadah that clarifies the words of the text in a way that fits those words" (*Bereishis* 3:8). That his commentary (first printed in Reggio di Calabria, 1475) is included in every edition of the *Chumash*, and more than 300 supercommentaries have been published probing his words, is a measure of Rashi's eminence.

In addition to his *peirush* on Chumash, Rashi wrote a comprehensive commentary on the Gemara, a masterpiece of clarity and brevity; without it, the Gemara would be a closed book. Rashi gently takes you by the hand, guiding you through the maze of complex forms of reasoning, obscure concepts, and knotty legal arguments. In clear and simple Hebrew, he clarifies the talmudic text line by line, anticipating the difficulties the student will encounter.

Rashi's Life and Legacy

Rashi (acronym for **R**abbi **Sh**elomoh ben **Y**itzchak) was born in Troyes, France, in 1040 c.e. and died in Troyes in 1105. He traced his ancestry to the tanna'im Rabbi Yochanan HaSandler and Hillel HaZaken, and back to David HaMelech. After received his early talmudic instruction from his father, Rashi went to Mainz, Germany to broaden his knowledge under Rabbi Yaakov ben Yakar, a disciple of Rabbeinu Gershon Meor Hagolah. Afterwards he studied at the yeshivah of Rabbi Yitzchak HaLevi in Worms. At the age of 25 he returned to his native Troyes where he founded a yeshivah that attracted the most gifted scholars of Western Europe.

A well-known anecdote relates that Rashi's parents were childless for many years. One day, his father found an exquisite jewel. When word of this find spread, a church dignitary tried forcing him to sell the stone to adorn a statue of their deity. Rashi's father refused to sell the stone for such a purpose, throwing it instead into the river. Afterwards, Eliyahu Hanavi appeared to him saying: "Since you forfeited a radiant gem for the sake of kiddush Hashem, you will be rewarded with the birth of a son who will illuminate the world with his Torah knowledge." A year later, his illustrious son Shelomoh was born.

Rashi had no sons. His daughters married outstanding Torah scholars: Their sons—Rashi's grandsons—were the great Tosafists: Rabbeinu Tam (R. Yaakov ben Meir) and Rashbam (R. Shmuel ben Meir).

It can be said without exaggeration that Rashi has been the foremost teacher of the Jewish people for the last 900 years. He truly merits the acronym of "Rashi"—**R**abban **SH**el **Y**israel, "Teacher of Yisrael."

May this translation of selected aggados of Rashi's commentary on the Torah whet your appetite for studying Torah and Talmud with the complete *peirush* of Rashi.

Avraham Yaakov Finkel
Kislev, 5769/'09

RASHI

ON THE TORAH

פירוש רש"י על התורה

BEREISHIS

SHEMOS

בראשית
BEREISHIS

THE CREATION OF HEAVEN AND EARTH

1:1 In the beginning, G-d created heaven and earth.

IN THE BEGINNING—Rabbi Yitzchak said: The Torah [was given primarily to teach us laws, therefore it] should begin with, *This month shall be for you the beginning of the months* (*Shemos* 12:2), the first law given to [the nation of] Yisrael.

Why does [the Torah] begin with, *In the beginning G-d created*? [The reason is expressed in the verse,] *He declared the power of His works to His people to give them the heritage of the nations* (*Tehillim* 111:6). If the nations of the world say to Yisrael, "You are robbers, because you took the lands of the Seven Nations [of Canaan] by force." Yisrael can respond, "The entire world belongs to the Holy One, blessed be He. He created it and gave it to whomever He saw fit. It was His will to give it to [the Seven Nations of Canaan], and it was His will to take it from them and give it to us."

IN THE BEGINNING G-D CREATED—[The literal translation of] this verse [is, "Because of the beginning, G-d created,"] which requires a Midrashic explanation. Our Rabbis explained: [G-d created the world] for the sake of the Torah, which is called, *The beginning of*

His way (*Mishlei* 8:22), and for the sake of Yisrael who is called, *The beginning of His harvest* (*Yirmeyah* 2:3).

G-D CREATED—[In the Hebrew text the word Elokim is used for G-d.] It does not say, "Hashem created,"[1] because initially He intended to create [the world with] the attribute of justice. When He realized the world would not exist, He prioritized the attribute of mercy, combining it with the attribute of justice. This [idea] is expressed in the verse, *On the day that Hashem Elokim made earth and heaven* (*Bereishis* 2:4), [where both Names are mentioned, and the Merciful Name of Hashem is placed before the Name Elokim, which means strict judge].

1:26 G-d said: "Let Us make man, with our image and likeness."

LET US MAKE MAN—This verse demonstrates the humility of the Holy One, blessed be He. Since man [was created] in the image of the angels, they might become jealous of him, therefore He sought their advice [to mollify them]. When G-d judges kings, He consults His assembly [of angels], as we find in connection with Achav. Michaiahu the prophet said to him, "*I have seen Hashem sitting upon His Throne, with all the hosts of heaven standing by Him, on His right and on His left* (1 *Melachim* 22:19)." Does G-d have a right and a left side? [We understand this to mean that] some angels leaned towards His right, recommending acquittal, and some leaned towards His left, pleading for a guilty verdict. Similarly, it says, *The matter is by decree of the angels, and the sentence is by the word of the holy ones* [i.e., angels] (*Daniel* 4:14). Here too, He asked permission from His Heavenly assembly [of angels], explaining, "Since there are angels in My image in heaven, if there are no [beings] in My image on earth, there will be jealousy in Creation."

---

1   The name Elokim represents the divine attribute of unmitigated justice; the name Hashem denotes the attribute of mercy.

LET US MAKE MAN—Although [the angels] did not help G-d create man and the phrase, *Let Us make man* gives heretics an opportunity to claim [that there is more than one deity, nevertheless,] the Torah does not restrain itself [and uses the term "Us"] to teach proper conduct and humility, that one of higher rank should consult and ask permission from lower ranking beings. Had the Torah said, "I will make man," we would not know that He spoke with His heavenly assembly [of angels, rather we would think that He reasoned] with Himself. The rebuttal [to the erroneous conclusion drawn by the heretics] is written in the next verse, where it states, *He created man* (1:27), not, "*They* created man."

1:31 G-d saw all that He had made, and behold, it was very good. It was evening, and it was morning, the sixth day.

THE SIXTH DAY—[The sixth day in the Hebrew text is, *Yom HaShishi*] *Yom HaShishi*—the sixth day—is written with an extra *hei* [whose numeric value is five], because G-d stipulated with His creations [that they would only endure] on condition that Yisrael accept the Five Books of the Torah.

Another explanation for [the *hei* of] *Yom hashishi*: All creation remained in a doubtful state until [the celebrated] *sixth day,* namely the sixth day [of the month] of Sivan, [the day the Torah was given].

2:2 G-d finished on the seventh day the work that He had done, He [thus] ceased on the seventh day from all the work that He had done.

G-D FINISHED ON THE SEVENTH DAY THE WORK THAT HE HAD DONE—Rabbi Shimon[2] says: [Man who is] flesh and blood cannot know precisely any point in time, [therefore] he must add from the secular to the holy. However, the Holy One, blessed be He, mea-

---

2   The Tanna Rabbi Shimon ben Yochai.

sures times and moments accurately entering into [the Shabbos] by a hairbreadth [exactly at the beginning of Shabbos], thus making it appear as if He finished His work in the seventh day itself. [That is why it says, *G-d finished on the seventh day the work that He had done*].

Another explanation: Before Shabbos the world was still missing rest. With the onset of Shabbos rest was created, and now the work [of creation] was finished and completed.

2:4 These are the chronicles of heaven and earth when they were created, on the day that Hashem G-d made earth and heaven.

WHEN THEY WERE CREATED—[The Hebrew word for, "When they were created" is, *behibare'am* a contraction of] *behei bare'am*, meaning: He created them with the letter *hei*, as it says, *For with G-d's Name Yud-Hei, Hashem formed the worlds* (*Yeshayah* 26:4). With these two letters [*yud* and *hei*] of the divine Name, He created two worlds [this world and the World to Come]. From our verse we learn that this world was created with the letter *hei*, hinting that the wicked will descend to the nether [world] to Gehinnom, like the letter *hei*, which is closed on all sides but open at the bottom for them to descend there. In other versions [the following is added:] Just as the letter *hei* is open at the bottom, so too, this world is open to those who return through *teshuvah*.

The World to Come was created with the letter *yud*, hinting that the righteous living at that time will be few in number, like the *yud* which is the smallest of all letters.

2:5 All the trees of the field were not yet on the earth, and all the herb of the field had not yet sprouted, for Hashem, Elokim, had not sent rain upon the earth, and there was no man to work the soil.

HASHEM, ELOKIM—Hashem is His Name; Elokim [means] He is the Ruler and Judge over everything. This combination always means—Hashem who is the Ruler and Judge.

2:7 And Hashem G-d formed the man from dust of the ground, and He blew into his nostrils the soul of life, and man became a living being.

HE FORMED—The word *Vayitzer*—and He formed—is written with two *yuds* alluding to two creations. He was created once for this world, and once for the revival of the dead. The word *vayitzer* is not written with two *yuds* by the creation of animals, since they will not be judged in time to come.

THE SIN OF EATING FROM THE TREE OF KNOWLEDGE

3:7 Then the eyes of both of them were opened and they realized that they were naked; they sewed together fig leaves and made themselves aprons.

FIG LEAVES—The [fig] tree from which they ate and with which [Adam and Chavah] sinned, became the agent through which the damage was repaired. Indeed, the other trees prevented them from taking their leaves.

Why was the name of the tree [with which they sinned] not -revealed? Because the Holy One, blessed be He, unwilling to cause pain to any creature, did not want [the tree] to be shamed, through people saying, "This is the one through which the world was punished."

3:9 Hashem G-d called out to the man and said to him; "Where are you?"

HASHEM G-D CALLED OUT TO THE MAN—G-d knew where he was, but [asked "Where are you?"] to open the conversation, so he should not be too startled to answer, [as would be the case] if he were punished suddenly. Similarly, He said to Kayin[3], *"Where is your brother Hevel?" (Bereishis* 4:9), and [He asked] Bilam, *Who are*

---

[3] After Kayin murdered Hevel.

these people with you?" (*Bamidbar* 22:9). [These questions were] to begin conversations. This was also true in the case of Chizkiyahu and the emissaries of Merodach-baladan (*Yeshayah* 39:3).[4]

KAYIN MURDERS HEVEL

4:9 Hashem said to Kayin: "Where is your brother, Hevel?" He replied, "I do not know. Am I my brother's keeper?"

WHERE IS YOUR BROTHER, HEVEL?—He began speaking gently, so Kayin would repent and admit, "I killed him, and I sinned to You."

THE FLOOD OF NOACH

6:6 Hashem reconsidered having made Man on earth, and He had heartfelt sadness.

HE HAD HEARTFELT SADNESS—He was saddened over the destruction of His handiwork, as in, *The king is saddened over his son* (2 *Shemuel* 19:3). I wrote this as a rebuttal to the heretics.

A gentile asked Rabbi Yehoshua ben Korcha, "Don't you admit that G-d foresees the future?"

"Yes I do," Rabbi Yehoshua replied.

"But it says, *He had heartfelt sadness!*" the gentile argued. [If G-d knows the future He should not have created man, rather than later regretting his creation!]

Rabbi Yehoshua replied, "Was a son ever born to you?"

"Yes," he said.

---

4   Yeshayah rebuked King Chizkiah for showing the treasures of the Beis Hamikdash to the messengers of Meradach-Maladan, king of Babylonia. He opened his reprimand saying, *"What did these men say, and from where did they come to you?"*

"And what did you do [when you heard the news]?" Rabbi Yehoshua asked.

"I rejoiced and made everyone else rejoice," replied the gentile.

"But did you not realize that he would eventually die?" Rabbi Yehoshua said.

"At the time of joy, let there be joy, and at a time of mourning, let there be mourning."

Replied Rabbi Yehoshua, "The Holy One, blessed be He, acts the same way. Although it was obvious to Him that ultimately they would sin, and He would destroy them, He did not refrain from creating them, for the sake of the righteous that were destined to descend from them.

נ ח

NOACH

6:9,10 These are the offspring of Noach. Noach was a righteous man, perfect in his generation. Noach walked with G-d. And Noach gave birth to three sons, Shem, Cham and Yefes.

THESE ARE THE OFFSPRING OF NOACH. NOACH WAS A RIGHTEOUS MAN—[Why does the Torah interrupt the genealogy of Noach with the mention that Noach was a righteous man?] Since the Torah mentions him, it tells his praise, as it says, *When mentioning a righteous man one blesses him* (*Mishlei* 10:7).

Another explanation: [Noach was a righteous man is mentioned immediately following, *These are the offspring of Noach,*] to teach us that the main posterity of the righteous are their good deeds.

6:14 Make for yourself an ark of gopher wood; make the ark with compartments, and coat it inside and out with pitch.

MAKE FOR YOURSELF—[G-d] has many ways of bringing relief and rescue. Why, then, did He burden Noach with building this [ark]? So the people of the generation [who perished in] the Flood, would see him working on [the ark] for one hundred and twenty years, and ask him, "What is the purpose of this?" He would answer, "The Holy One, blessed be He, is planning to bring a flood on the world." Perhaps they might repent.

7:1 Hashem said to Noach, "Come into the Ark, you and your whole household, for it is you that I have seen to be righteous before Me in this generation."

IT IS YOU THAT I HAVE SEEN TO BE RIGHTEOUS BEFORE ME IN THIS GENERATION—It does not say, "righteous, perfect before Me" [as in verse 6:9]. From here we learn that we mention [only] part of a person's praise in his presence [as here, where G-d speaks directly to Noach;] and all of it in his absence.

8:1 G-d [Elokim] remembered Noach and all the beasts and all the cattle that were with him in the ark, and G-d caused a spirit to pass over the earth, and the waters subsided.

G-D [ELOKIM] REMEMBERED—The Name [Elokim] represents the divine attribute of strict Justice, yet it was converted into the attribute of Mercy through the prayer of the righteous. Conversely, the evil deeds of the wicked turn the attribute of Mercy into the attribute of Justice, as it says [above], *Hashem saw that the wickedness of man was great . . . and Hashem said, "I will blot out . . ."* (6:5), although the Name Hashem usually represents the attribute of Mercy.

8:11 The dove returned to him in the evening, and behold, a plucked olive leaf was in its mouth.

A PLUCKED [*TARAF*] OLIVE LEAF WAS IN ITS MOUTH—The Midrash explains that the word *taraf* is often used as an expression of food [as in *Mishlei* 31:15 and *Malachi* 3:10] and *in its mouth* means speech. [The dove] said, "May my food be as bitter as an olive in the hand of the Holy One, blessed be He, rather than sweet as honey in the hands of [man, who is only] flesh and blood." [I would rather receive bitter-tasting food directly from G-d, than sweet delicacies through man.]

Noach Sacrifices after the Flood

8:21 G-d smelled the appeasing fragrance [of the sacrifice], and G-d said to Himself, "Never again will I curse the soil because of man, for the inclination of man's heart is evil from his youth. I will never again strike down all life as I have just done."

From his youth—[The Hebrew for "From his youth" is,] *Min'urav*, which is written without a *vav*, [which is derived from the word *na'or*, "to stir"], implying that from the time the embryo stirs to emerge from his mother's womb the evil impulse is placed in him.

Covering the Nakedness of Noach

9:23 Shem and Yefes took a cloak and placed it on both their shoulders. Walking backward, they covered their father's nakedness. They faced away from him and did not see their father naked.

Shem and Yefes took [*VAYIKACH*]—It does not say *vayikchu* ["they took"], but *vayikach* ["he took"], teaching us that Shem exerted himself more than Yefes to fulfill the commandment [of honoring his father.] Therefore, his offspring [Yisrael] merited a *tallis* with *tzitzis*, while Yefes [only] merited burial for his sons, as it says, *I will assign Gog*[5] *a burial site here in Yisrael* (*Yechezkel* 39:11). However, Cham disgraced his father, so it says about his offspring, *So will the king of Assyria lead away the captivity of Egypt and the exile of Kush—young and old—naked and barefoot, with exposed buttocks, the nakedness of Egypt* (*Yeshayah* 20:4).

---

5   Gog, prince of the land of Magog, is one of the sons of Yefes (*Bereishis* 10:2).

10:25 Eiver had two sons. The name of the first was Peleg, because the world became divided in his days. His brother's name was Yoktan.

YOKTAN—[The name Yoktan is derived from *katan*, "small." He was called Yoktan] because he was humble and considered himself small. Therefore he merited all these [thirteen] families.

THE TOWER OF BAVEL

11:5 G-d descended to see the city and the town that the sons of man had built.

G-D DESCENDED TO SEE—It was not necessary for Him to descend, but He did so in order to teach judges not to condemn a defendant until they review [the case] and understand it.

THE SONS OF MAN—[Why does it say the sons of man?] Could they have been the sons of donkeys and camels? [They are referred to as] the sons of Adam, the first man, who [was ungrateful,] denying the goodness he received from G-d. He said, *The woman who you gave [to be] with me, she gave me the fruit of the tree and I ate* (*Bereishis* 3:12). These [people, who built the Tower,] were also ungrateful, rebelling against the One who bestowed an abundance of goodness on them, saving them from the Flood.

11:7 Come, let Us descend and confuse their speech, so that one person will not understand the other's speech.

LET US DESCEND—["Let us descend," rather than, "I will descend",] teaches that He [first] consulted His [heavenly] court, out of His exceptional humility.

11:9 He named it Bavel, because this was the place where G-d confused the world's language. It was from there that G-d dispersed [humanity] over all the face of the earth.

IT WAS FROM THERE THAT G-D DISPERSED [HUMANITY]—[The generation of the Flood was destroyed, whereas the generation of the Dispersion was not destroyed.] Which sins were worse, those of the generation of the Flood or those of the generation of the Dispersion? The generation of the Flood did not stretch forth their hands against G-d, whereas the generation of the Dispersion stretched forth their hands against G-d, waging war against Him, nevertheless, the former were drowned while the latter did not perish from the world. Since the generation of the Flood robbed, and there was discord between them, they perished, however [the generation of the Dispersion] treated each other with love and friendship, as it says, *The entire earth had one language and uniform words* (11:1). From here we learn that conflict is hated and peace is great.

11:28 [Avram's brother] Haran, died in the living presence of his father, Terach, in the land of his birth, Ur Kasdim.

IN THE LIVING PRESENCE OF HIS FATHER TERACH—[Means, he died] during his father's lifetime. The *Midrash Aggadah* tells us that [Haran] died because of his father. After Avram shattered his idols, Terach brought Avram to Nimrod. Nimrod cast Avram into a fiery furnace, while Haran sat still [biding his time,] thinking, "If Avram wins, I am on his side; if Nimrod wins, I am on his side." When Avram was saved they said to Haran, "With whom do you side?" Haran replied, "I side with Avram." They cast him into the fiery furnace, and he was burned. Therefore it is called *ur Kasdim*, [because *ur* means fire and Haran died in the fire of the *Kasdim*].

לֶךְ לְךָ
LECH LECHA

———◆———

12:1 G-d said to Avram, "Go for yourself from your land, from your birthplace, and from your father's house, to the land that I will show you."

TO THE LAND THAT I WILL SHOW YOU—G-d did not reveal the land to Avram right away, in order to make it dear in his eyes, [for the anticipation of the unknown heightens one's desire.]

Another reason: To give him reward for each separate command. In the same vein, it says, *Your son, your only son, whom you love, Yitzchak* (*Bereishis* 22:2), and, *on one of the mountains that I will designate to you* (ibid.), and, *Call out against her the proclamation that I will tell you* (*Yonah* 3:2) [In all these cases G-d did not reveal the intended subject right away.]

12:5 Avram took his wife Sarai, his nephew Lot, and all their belongings, as well as the people they had acquired in Charan. They left heading for Canaan, and they came to the land of Canaan.

THE PEOPLE THEY HAD ACQUIRED IN CHARAN—[The literal translation is "the people they had made in Charan",] which means, the people they brought under the wings of the *Shechinah* [converting them from idol worship to belief in G-d]. Avraham converted the men, and Sarah converted the women. Because the Torah considers it as if they had made them, it says, "The people they had made."

12:10 There was a famine in the land. Avram went down to Egypt to stay there for a while, since the famine was very severe in the land.

THERE WAS A FAMINE IN THE LAND—[The famine was] only in that land, to test whether Avram would question the words of the Holy One, blessed be He, who ordered him to go to the Land of Canaan, and was now forcing him to leave it.

AVRAHAM WAGES WAR AGAINST THE FOUR KINGS

14:15 He divided [his forces] against them [and attacked] that night—he and his servants. He attacked and pursued [the invaders] as far as Chovah, which is to the left of Damesek.

HE DIVIDED [HIS FORCES] AGAINST THEM THAT NIGHT—The *Midrash Aggadah* says, that the night itself was divided. In the first half of the night a miracle was performed for Avram, [and he defeated his enemies], while the second half [of the night] was preserved for the [miracle of the Exodus, which occurred at] midnight in Egypt.

THE COVENANT BETWEEN THE PARTS

15:10 Avram brought all these for Him. He split them in half, placing one half opposite the other. The bird, however, he did not split.

THE BIRD, HOWEVER, HE DID NOT SPLIT—The idol-worshipping nations are compared to bulls, rams, and goats, as it says, *Many bulls surround me* (*Tehillim* 22:13), and, *The two-horned ram that you saw [symbolizes] the kings of Media and Persia* (*Daniel* 8:20), and, *The he-goat [symbolizes] the kingdom of Greece* (ibid. v.21). However, Yisrael is likened to a young dove, as it says, *My dove in the clefts of the rock* (*Shir Hashirim* 2:14). He split the animals, implying that the nations will gradually fade away. *The bird, however, he did not split,* suggesting that Yisrael will exist forever.

15:11 Vultures descended on the carcasses, and Avram blew them away.

BUT AVRAM BLEW THEM AWAY—This alludes to the fact that David the son of Yishai will try to destroy [the idolatrous nations], but Heaven will not permit him [to do so] until the coming of King Mashiach.

16:1 Avram's wife Sarai had not borne him any children. She had an Egyptian slave-girl by the name of Hagar.

AN EGYPTIAN SLAVE-GIRL—She was Pharaoh's daughter. When [Pharaoh] saw the miracles performed for Sarah, he said, "Better that my daughter be a slave-girl in this household than a mistress in another household.

The Commandment of Circumcision

17:1 Avram was 99 years old. G-d appeared to him and said, "I am G-d the Almighty. Walk before me, and be perfect."

I AM G-D THE ALMIGHTY—[The Hebrew word for "the almighty" is, *Shad-dai*, which translates as "that is sufficient" thus denoting:] I am the One whose G-dliness is sufficient [to fulfill the needs] of every creature. Therefore, [you can] walk before Me, and I will be your G-d and your Protector. Whenever this Name appears in

Tanach, it means "He is sufficient," with each case being interpreted according to its context.

WALK BEFORE ME—The Targum translates: Serve Me; attach yourself to My service.

AND BE PERFECT—This command follows the command [of "Walk
before Me." In addition to attaching yourself to My service, I command you to *Be perfect*] passing all My trials.

According to the Midrash, the phrase *Walk before Me,* refers to
the commandment of circumcision. [The verse concludes,] *thereby
you will be perfect,* for as long as you have a foreskin I consider you
imperfect.

Another explanation of, *Be perfect* is: Until now you had no control over the five organs [which tempt man to sin]: your two eyes,
your two ears, and your male organ. [Through the covenant of circumcision I will give you control over your base instincts. I will
change your name from Avram to Avraham] adding the letter [*hei,*
whose numerical value is five,] to your name, bringing the numeric value of your name to 248,[6] the number of all human organs,
[demonstrating that you have control over all of them.]

17:8 To you and your offspring I will give the land where
you are now living as a foreigner. The whole land of
Canaan shall be [your] eternal heritage, and I will be a G-d to
them.

THE WHOLE LAND OF CANAAN SHALL BE [YOUR] ETERNAL HER-
ITAGE, AND I WILL BE A G-D TO THEM.—I will be a G-d to them
when they live in the land, but one who lives outside [Eretz
Yisrael], is considered as if he has no G-d.

17:19 G-d said: "Still, your wife Sarah will give birth to a
son. You must name him Yitzchak. I will keep My

---

6   alef=1; beis=2; reish=200; hei=5; mem=40. 1+2+200+5=248

covenant with him as an eternal treaty, for his descendants after him.

YOU MUST NAME HIM YITZCHAK—Which alludes to *tzechok*—the laughter [and joy of Avraham when he heard that he would have a son from Sara (17:17)].

Some say [the name Yitzchak, which is written *yud, tzadi, ches, kuf* with numerical values of 10-90-8-100], alludes to [*yud* (10)] the ten trials Avraham passed; [*tzadi* (90)] the ninety years of Sarah [when she gave birth]; [*ches* (8)] the eighth day on which he was circumcised; and [*kuf* (100)] the one hundred years of Avraham's age [when Yitzchak was born].

וירא

VA'YEIRA

———⊶⟨◉⟩⊷———

18:1 G-d appeared to [Avraham] in the Plains of Mamre while he was sitting at the entrance of the tent in the hottest part of the day.

HE WAS SITTING—Although this is read, "He was sitting," the actual text says, "he sat." Though he was sitting, he wished to stand [when G-d appeared to him]. Said the Holy One, blessed be He, to him, "You sit, while I stand." This will signal your children that in time to come I will stand in the congregation of their judges, while they sit," as it says, *G-d stands in the divine assembly* (*Tehillim* 82:1).

18:8 Abraham fetched some cream and milk and the calf that he prepared, and he placed it before them.[7] He stood over them as they ate under the tree.

AS THEY ATE—[Although angels don't eat,] they appeared to be eating. From here we learn that one should not deviate from local custom.

---

7   The angels who appeared to him as guests.

THE DESTRUCTION OF SEDOM

18:16 The strangers got up from their places and they gazed at Sedom, [planning its destruction.] Avraham went with them to send them on their way.

AND THEY GAZED AT SEDOM—[The Hebrew word for "And they gazed" is, *Vayashkifu*.] The word *hashkafah* ["gaze"] in Tanach always refers to punishment, except for the verse *Hashkifah—Look down from Your holy habitation [and bless Your Nation Yisrael]* (*Devarim* 26:15), [which refers to the tithe of the poor]. The power of gifts to the poor is so great it converts the divine attribute of Anger, [indicated by the word *hashkifah,*] to Mercy.

18:19 I have given him special attention because he commands his children and his household after him, to keep G-d's way, doing charity and justice, so that G-d will bring on Avraham everything He promised.

SO THAT G-D WILL BRING ON AVRAHAM—He commanded his sons to keep G-d's way so that G-d will bring on Avraham everything He promised. Note: It does not say, "G-d will bring on the house of Avraham" but "G-d will bring on Avraham." From here we learn that whoever raises a righteous son is considered as though he did not die.

THE BIRTH OF YITZCHAK

21:1 G-d had remembered Sarah as He said He would, and G-d did what He promised for Sarah.

G-D HAD REMEMBERED SARAH—This section was placed next to [the section of the Torah where Avraham prayed that Avimelech be cured,] teaching that whoever begs for mercy for his friend, is answered first, if he himself needs the same thing. As it says, *Avraham prayed to G-d, and G-d healed Avimelech* (*Bereishis* 20:17), followed by, *G-d [had] remembered Sarah*, meaning, He remembered her even before He healed Avimelech.

21:33 [Avraham] planted an eishel in Be'er Sheva, and there he called in the name of Hashem, the G-d of the world.

[AVRAHAM] PLANTED AN EISHEL IN BE'ER SHEVA—Rav and Shmuel disagree on the meaning of eishel. One says he planted an orchard to bring fruits for his guests to eat. And one says he opened an inn serving fruits to his guests . . .

THERE HE CALLED IN THE NAME OF HASHEM, THE G-D OF THE WORLD—Through this *eishel* the name of the Holy One, blessed be He, was called "G-d of the whole world," for after [the wayfarers] ate and drank, he would say to them, "Bless the One whose food you have eaten. Though you think you have eaten my food, [this is not so,] rather, you have eaten from the One who created the world through His word."

YITZCHAK BROUGHT AS A SACRIFICE

22:1 It came to pass after *these* events, that G-d tested Avraham [by asking him to sacrifice his son Yitzchock.] He said, "Avraham!" [Avraham] answered, "Here I am."

AFTER THESE EVENTS—[The Hebrew for "These events" is *Hadevarim ha'eleh*. The literal translation of *hadevarim* is "words."] Some of our Sages say this verse is to be interpreted: After the Satan said words criticizing Avraham [before G-d] saying, "Avraham made an entire feast [on the day Yitzchak was weaned,] yet he did not offer You even one bull or ram." [G-d] replied: "He made the feast only in honor of his son. Were I were to tell him, 'Sacrifice [your son] before Me,' he would not withhold him."

Some say: "After the words of Yishmael" who boasted to Yitzchak that he was circumcised at the age of thirteen without protesting, [whereas Yitzchak was circumcised on the eighth day of his life when he could not protest]. Yitzchak said to him, "You think to frighten me by challenging me about obeying G-d's will with one organ! If the Holy One, blessed be He, were to say to me, 'Sacrifice yourself before Me,' I would not protest."

"HERE I AM"—This is how the devout reply. It is an expression of humility and readiness.

22:12 He said, "Do not stretch forth your hand to [harm] the boy. Do not do anything to him. For now I know that you fear G-d. You have not withheld your only son from Me."

FOR NOW I KNOW—Now I have a response to Satan and the nations who wonder why I have such love for you. Now I am justified, for they see *that you fear G-d*.

22:13 Avraham lifted up his eyes and saw a ram caught by its horns in a thicket. Avraham went and took the ram, and offered it as a burnt offering instead of his son.

INSTEAD OF HIS SON—Since it says, *and he offered it as a burnt offering*, nothing is missing in the text. Why does it continue and say, *instead of his son*? Over every act he performed [in offering the ram] he prayed, "May it be Your will that this be considered as if it were being done to my son. [May it be] as if my son were slaughtered, as if his blood were sprinkled, as if his flesh were flayed, as if my son were burned and reduced to ashes."

שׂרה

CHAYEI SARAH

———◦(((◦)))◦———

FINDING A WIFE FOR YITZCHAK

24:7 Hashem, the G-d of heaven, who took me away from my father's house and from the land of my birth, and who spoke to me and made an oath saying, "To your offspring I will give this land," He will send His angel before you, and you will find a wife for my son there.

HASHEM, THE G-D OF HEAVEN—He did not say, "And the G-d of the earth," whereas above (verse 3) he said, *I will bind you by an oath to Hashem, the G-d of the heaven and the G-d of the earth.* He told him, "Now He is the G-d of heaven and earth, because I have made him familiar in the mouths of the people, however, when He took me from my father's house, He was only the G-d of the heaven, not the G-d of the earth. Because mankind did not acknowledge Him, His name was not familiar on the earth.

24:10 The servant took ten of his master's camels, bringing along the best of his master's possessions. He set off and went to Aram Naharayim, to the city of Nachor.

TEN OF HIS MASTER'S CAMELS—They were clearly recognizable as his master's camels, because they went out muzzled, to prevent them from grazing in fields belonging to others.

24:42 I came today to the well, and I said, "O Hashem, G-d of my master Avraham, if you will, grant success to this mission that I am undertaking."

I CAME TODAY TO THE WELL—Today I left, and today I arrived. From here we learn that the earth leaped toward him [helping him reach his destination quickly].

Rabbi Akiva said: The ordinary conversation of the servants of the Patriarchs is more beloved by G-d than the Torah [discourses] of their sons. Thus the section dealing with Eliezer's [mission] is repeated twice in the Torah, whereas many fundamentals of the Torah were given only through allusions.

24:67 Yitzchak brought her into the tent of Sarah his mother. He married Rivkah, she became his wife, and he loved her. Yitzchak was then consoled for the loss of his mother.

INTO THE TENT OF SARAH HIS MOTHER—When he brought her into the tent, behold, she was as Sarah, his mother! For as long as Sarah was alive, a candle burned from one Shabbos eve to the next, there was blessing in the dough, and a [protective] cloud hovered over the tent. When she died, they ceased, however, when Rivkah entered [the tent] they returned.

תולדות

TOLEDOS

———◦◉◦———

YAAKOV AND EISAV

25:25,26 The first one emerged reddish, completely covered with hair like a hairy garment, and they called him Eisav. Afterwards his brother emerged, with his hand grasping Eisav's heel, and he named him Yaakov. Yitzchak was sixty years old when they were born.

EISAV'S HEEL—This is a sign that [Eisav] will not manage to complete his reign until [Yaakov] rises up and takes it from him.

26:34 When Eisav was forty years old he married Yehudis, daughter of Be'eri the Hittite, and Basemas, daughter of Eilon the Hittite.

FORTY YEARS OLD—Eisav is compared to a swine, as it says, *The swine of the forest [Eisav] ravages it* (*Tehillim* 80:14). When the swine lies down it stretches out its hoofs, as if to say, "See, I am a kosher animal."[8] So too, the [chiefs of Eisav] rob and plunder yet pretend to be respectable. During the first forty years [of his life]

---

8   All animals that have split hoofs and chew the cud are kosher. The swine has split hoofs, but does not chew the cud. Thus, in spite of its split hoofs, it is a non-kosher animal.

Eisav abducted wives from their husbands, violating them. When he was forty years old, he said, "My father married at forty, I too, will do the same."

27:1 Yitzchak had grown old and his eyesight was fading. He summoned his elder son Eisav, and said to him, "My son," and he replied, "Here I am."

HIS EYESIGHT WAS FADING—Damaged by the smoke of the [wives of Eisav] who burned incense to the idols.

Another explanation: When Yitzchak was bound on the altar with his father about to slaughter him, the heavens opened, and the ministering angels saw him and wept. Their tears fell on Yitzchak's eyes causing them to become dim.

A third explanation: [His eyesight faded] to enable Yaakov to take the blessings.

וַיֵּצֵא

VAYETZEI

———◆———

28:10 Yaakov left Beersheva and headed toward Charan.

YAAKOV LEFT BEERSHEVA—It should have said, *Yaakov headed toward Charan*. Why is his departure mentioned? This teaches us that a righteous man's departure makes an impression on the city, for while a righteous man is in a place, he is its splendor and majesty. When he departs, its splendor and majesty depart. So too, it says about Naomi and Ruth, *She left the place where she had been* (*Ruth* 1:7).

28:11 He came to the place and spent the night there because the sun had already set. He took some stones from there and placed them at his head, and there he lay down to sleep.

AND PLACED THEM AT HIS HEAD—He arranged them in the form of a trench around his head because he was afraid of wild beasts. [The stones] began to quarrel with each other, each one saying, "Let this righteous man place his head on me." Immediately, the Holy One, blessed be He, made them into one stone. That is why [in a later verse] it refers to it as one stone; *He took the stone he had placed at his head* (ibid. 28:18).

AND THERE HE LAY DOWN TO SLEEP—The word "there" denotes an exclusion, telling us that [only] in that place he lay down, but during the fourteen years he spent as a student in the academy of Eiver he did not lie down at night, because he was engrossed in Torah study.

28:15 I am with you. I will protect you wherever you go and bring you back to this land. I will not forsake you until I have done what I have spoken concerning you.

WHAT I HAVE SPOKEN CONCERNING YOU—That which I promised Avraham concerning his offspring, I promised regarding you, and not regarding Eisav. I did not say to [Avraham], "For Yitzchak will be called your offspring," [which would mean that all of Yitzchak's descendants—including Eisav—would be regarded as Avraham's descendants.] Rather I said, *for from among Yitzchak will be called your offspring,* [which means that] not all of Yitzchak's [descendants will be called Avraham's descendants, thus excluding Eisav].

YAAKOV MARRIES RACHEL AND LEAH

29:17 Leah's eyes were tender, while Rachel was beautiful in form and beautiful in appearance.

LEAH'S EYES WERE TENDER—From weeping, for she thought she was destined [to marry] Eisav. People said, "Rivkah has two sons, and Lavan two daughters. The older daughter [Leah] will be for the older son [Eisav], and the younger daughter [Rachel] will be for the younger son [Yaakov].

29:25 In the morning [Yaakov discovered] that it was Leah. He said to Lavan, "How could you do this to me? Didn't I work with you for Rachel? Why did you cheat me?

IN THE MORNING [YAAKOV DISCOVERED] THAT IT WAS LEAH—But at night Yaakov did not realize that she was Leah, because Yaakov [fearing Lavan's deception] had given certain [identifying] signs to Rachel. When Rachel saw they were bringing Leah, she said, "Now my sister [who does not know the signs] will be humiliated," and readily gave her the signs.

30:1 Rachel realized that she was not bearing any children to Yaakov. Rachel became jealous of her sister and said to Yaakov, "Give me children! If not, let me die!"

RACHEL BECAME JEALOUS OF HER SISTER—She envied her good deeds. She said, "Were she not more righteous than I, she would not have merited having children."

31:3 Hashem said to Yaakov, "Go back to your birthplace in the land of your fathers and I will be with you."

GO BACK TO YOUR BIRTHPLACE IN THE LAND OF YOUR FATHERS— And there I will be with you, but as long as you are associated with [Lavan,] the unclean one, it is impossible to make My Presence rest on you.

31:24 Hashem appeared to Lavan the Aramean at night in a dream, and said, "Be very careful not to say anything good or bad, to Yaakov."

GOOD OR BAD—All the good of the wicked is considered bad for the righteous. [That is why G-d warned him not to say even something he considered good for Yaakov.]

וישלח
VAYISHLACH

<hr style="width:30%"/>

YAAKOV PREPARES FOR AN ENCOUNTER WITH EISAV

32:5 [Yaakov] instructed [his agents] to deliver the following message, "So shall you say to my master Eisav, 'I stayed with Lavan, and have delayed my return until now.'"

I STAYED WITH LAVAN—The [Hebrew word for stayed, *garti*, has the numeric value of 613[9]]. Yaakov implied: Although I stayed with the wicked Lavan, I kept the 613 commandments [of the Torah], not learning from his evil deeds.

32:9 He said, "If Eisav comes and attacks one camp, at least the other camp will survive."

AT LEAST THE OTHER CAMP WILL SURVIVE—Even against [Eisav's] will, for I will wage war against him. [Yaakov] prepared himself in three ways: with a gift, with prayer, and for war. With a gift, as it says, *He sent the gift ahead of him* (32:22); with prayer, as it says, *G-d of my father Avraham* (32:10); for war, as it says, *the other camp will survive.*

<hr style="width:30%"/>

9   *Gimel*=3; *reish*=200; *tav*=400; *yud*=10

32:11 I have become unworthy from all the kindness and faith that you have shown me. [When I left home] I crossed the Yardein with only my staff, and now I have enough for two camps.

I HAVE BECOME UNWORTHY FROM ALL THE KINDNESS—The merits [I have earned for my good deeds] have diminished because of the kindnesses and the truth You have shown me. I am afraid that perhaps since you promised me all this, I have become tainted with sin, and therefore will be delivered into Eisav's hands.

YAAKOV BATTLES WITH THE GUARDIAN ANGEL OF EISAV

32:29 He [the Guardian angel of Eisav] said, "Your name will no longer be called Yaakov, but Yisrael, since you have become great before G-d and man, and you have won."

YOUR NAME WILL NO LONGER BE CALLED YAAKOV—It will no longer be said that you received the blessings through trickery and deception [as the name Yaakov, which comes from the word *akeivah*, implies], rather [you received them] with honor and candor. Ultimately, the Holy One, blessed be He, will reveal Himself to you in Beth-el and change your name. There He will bless you, and I, [the angel,] will be there to confirm that you are entitled [to that name].

32:30 Yaakov asked saying, "Tell me your name?" And [the angel] said, "Why do you ask my name?" He then blessed [Yaakov] there.

WHY DO YOU ASK MY NAME?—[The angel replied,] "We [angels] have no set names. Our names change according to the service we are commanded to do and the mission on which we are sent.

33:4 Eisav ran to meet him. He hugged him [Yaakov,] and, throwing himself on his shoulders, he kissed him, and they cried.

HE KISSED HIM—The word "he kissed him" are marked with dots on every letter. The *Baraisa* in *Sifrei* records different opinions about [the meaning of these dots]. Some interpret the dots to indicate that he did not kiss him wholeheartedly. Rabbi Shimon bar Yochai said, "We have a time-honored tradition that Eisav hates Yaakov. However, [the dots tell us that] at this moment, his compassion was aroused and he kissed him wholeheartedly."

36:6 Eisav took his wives, his sons, his daughters, and all the members of his household; his herds, his animals and all his possession she acquired in the Land of Canaan, and he went to a [different] land because of his brother Yaakov.

HE WENT TO A [DIFFERENT] LAND BECAUSE OF HIS BROTHER YAAKOV. The *Midrash,* explains that there was a promissory note based on the verse, *your offspring will be strangers in a land that is not theirs for 400 years* (*Bereishis* 15:13) which Yitzchak's descendants had to pay. Eisav said, "I will go away from here. I want neither a share in the gift of the land given to Yitzchock—nor in the payment of the promissory note [which would make me liable to be strangers for 400 years]." He also left because he felt shame that he had sold his birthright.

36:12 Timna became the concubine of Eisav's son Elifaz and she bore Amalek for Elifaz. All these are the descendants of Eisav's wife Adah.

TIMNA BECAME THE CONCUBINE—[This passage depicts] the honor of Avraham, showing how eager people were to attach themselves to his descendants. Timna was a daughter of a chieftain, as it says, *the sister of Lotan was Timna* (32:22). Lotan was a chieftains of Seir, ruling the Chorites who lived there before [Eisav settled there]. [Despite her royal ancestry] she said, "Although I am not worthy of marrying you, I wish to be your concubine."

וישב

VAYEISHEV

———◦(◉)◦———

YOSEF IS SOLD BY HIS BROTHERS

37:1,2 Yaakov settled in the land where his father had lived, in the land Canaan. These are the generations of Yaakov. Yosef was seventeen years old, and as a lad would tend the sheep with his brothers, the sons of Bilhah and Zilpah, his father's wives. And Yosef brought bad reports to his father about them.

YAAKOV SETTLED—The [previous] text described Eisav's settlements and his generations briefly, because they were neither respectable nor important [enough] to specify in detail how they settled, the order of their wars, and how they drove out the Chorites. [By contrast,] the Torah records the settlements of Yaakov and his generation, and all the events leading up to this at length, since they were important. Similarly, the verses about the ten generations from Adam to Noach merely say so-and-so begat so-and-so, but [the Torah] deals with Noach at length. The ten generations from Noach to Avraham are also discussed only briefly, but Avraham is dealt with at length. This may be compared to a pearl that fell into the sand. A person searches in the sand, sifting it with a sieve until he finds the pearl. When he finds it, he throws away the pebbles and keeps the pearl. [The pearl represents Yaakov, the sand represents mankind, and Eisav and his entourage are the pebbles.]

YAAKOV SETTLED—Another interpretation: A flax dealer's camels loaded with flax [once] entered [a town]. The local blacksmith wondered, "How will all this flax pass [through the narrow gate?]" A wise man answered, "One spark emanating from your bellows will burn all of it." So too, seeing all the chieftains of Eisav mentioned above,[10] Yaakov wondered, "Who can overpower all of these?"

[The answer to Yaakov's question] is contained in the following verse, *These are the generations of Yaakov, Yosef.* For it says, *The house of Yaakov shall be fire, and the house of Yosef a flame, and the house of Eisav shall become stubble (Ovadiah 1:18).* One spark emanating from Yosef will destroy and consume them all. From an old Rashi.

YAAKOV SETTLED IN THE LAND—Another interpretation: Yaakov wished to settle in tranquility, [but] the troubles of Yosef beset him. [When] the righteous want to settle in tranquility, the Holy One, blessed be He, says, "The righteous [think] that [the bliss] prepared for them in the World to Come is not enough; they wish to dwell in tranquility even in this world." [Being inordinate, their wish is not fulfilled.]

37:25 The brothers [threw Yosef into a pit and then] sat down and ate a meal. When they looked up they saw an Arab caravan coming from Gilad. Their camels were carrying spices, balm, and lotus, transporting them to Egypt. [The brothers then decided to sell Yosef to the Arabs.]

THEIR CAMELS WERE CARRYING SPICES, BALM, AND LOTUS—Why does the text publicize their cargo? To teach us the reward of the righteous. Usually Arabs carry only naphtha and tar, which have an offensive odor, but it was arranged for [Yosef that they carry] spices, so he should not be troubled by a foul odor.

---

10 *Bereishis* 36:15-19, 40-43.

YEHUDAH AND TAMAR

38:23 Yehudah[11] replied, "Let her keep [the security,] lest we become a laughingstock. I tried to send her the kid, but you could not find her."

I TRIED TO SEND HER THE KID—Since Yehudah had deceived his father with a kid in whose blood he dipped Yosef's coat, he too, was deceived with a kid.

38:25 When she was being taken out, she sent [the security] to her father-in-law with the message, "I am pregnant by the man who is the owner of these articles." She then said, "Please recognize to whom the signet ring, cloak, and staff, belong."

SHE SENT [THE SECURITY] TO HER FATHER-IN-LAW—She did not want to embarrass him saying, "By you I am pregnant," therefore [she said,] "I am pregnant by the man who is the owner of these articles." She thought, "If he admits [that he is the father,] fine. If not, let them burn me, rather than I shame him in public." From here [our Rabbis] said, "It is better for a person to be cast into a fiery furnace rather than shame his fellow in public."

40:1 After these events[12], the Egyptian king's wine steward and baker sinned against their master, against the king of Egypt.

AFTER THESE EVENTS—Because that cursed woman [Potiphar's wife] had accustomed the people to defame the righteous man [Yosef], the Holy One, blessed be He, caused these [two royal servants] to sin so people would turn [their attention] to them rather than Yosef. Additionally [they were imprisoned] so relief would come to the righteous man through them.

---

11 Yehudah promised Tamar a kid for her wages. She took a security from him, but he was then unable to find her.

12 Yosef was imprisoned after being falsely accused of molesting his master's wife.

מ ק ץ
MIKEITZ

———◦◉◦———

43:14 May G-d Al-mighty grant you mercy before the man and he will send your other brother along with Binyamin. If I must lose my children, then I will lose them.

MAY G-D AL-MIGHTY—At this point you lack nothing but prayer, therefore, I am praying for you.

MAY G-D AL-MIGHTY [*SHA-DAI*]—[The word *Sha-dai* is a contraction of *Sha* and *dai*,] which means, "Whose gift of mercy is sufficient, and who has sufficient power to grant it." The *Midrash* explains it as follows: May He, who [when the heaven and earth were expanding boundlessly during creation,] said "*dai*—enough!" to the world, say "enough!" to my troubles, for I have not enjoyed tranquility since my youth. I have endured the trouble of [living with] Lavan's [treachery], the trouble of Eisav [who wanted to kill me], the trouble of Rachel [who died in childbirth], the trouble of Dinah [who was kidnapped and molested by Shechem], the trouble of Yosef [who is missing], the trouble of Shimon [who is imprisoned in Egypt], and the trouble of Binyamin [whom I must send there].

ויגש
VAYIGASH

———◆———

YAAKOV AND HIS FAMILY GO DOWN TO EGYPT

46:26 Thus, the number of people who came to Egypt with Yaakov, those who descended from him, was 66, not counting the wives of Yaakov's sons.

THUS, THE NUMBER OF PEOPLE WHO CAME TO EGYPT—[The Hebrew for, "the number of people" is, *kol nefesh*.] I found [the following] in *Vayikra Rabbah* (4:6): Eisav's family numbered sixteen individuals, and the Torah calls them *nafshos beiso*, "the souls of his family" (*Bereishis* 36:6) using the plural, because they worshipped many gods. Yaakov had seventy souls, but the Torah calls them *nefesh* ["soul," using the singular], because they all worshipped one G-d.

וַיְחִי

VA'YECHI

YAAKOV'S INSTRUCTIONS ON HIS DEATHBED

47:29 When the time drew near for Yisrael to die, he called his son Yosef and said to him, "If I have found favor in your eyes, place your hand under my thigh. Act toward me with kindness and truth, and do not bury me in Egypt."

KINDNESS AND TRUTH—Kindness that is done toward the dead is true kindness, for one does not expect any payment, [from the dead.]

47:31 [Yaakov] said, "Swear to me." [Yosef] made an oath to him, and Yisrael bowed down on the head of the bed.

YISRAEL BOWED DOWN ON THE HEAD OF THE BED—He turned himself to the side of the *Shechinah*. From here [it can be inferred] that the *Shechinah* is at the head of a sick person.

48:7 When I was coming from Padan, [your mother] Rachel died on me. It was in Canaan, a short distance before we came to Efras. I buried her there along the road to Efras, which is Beis Lechem.

WHEN I WAS COMING FROM PADAN—I am troubling you to bury me
in the land of Canaan, although I did not do so for your mother,
who died near Beis Lechem.

I BURIED HER THERE—I did not even take her to Beis Lechem,
bringing her into the land. I know that in your heart you reproach
me for this, but you should know that I buried her there on G-d's
command, so she could assist her children. When Nevuzeraddan
will exile them and they pass there, Rachel will came out of her
grave, weeping and begging mercy for them, as it says, *A voice is
heard on high, wailing and bitter weeping, Rachel is weeping for her
children* (*Yirmeyah* 31:14). And the Holy One, blessed be He, answers her, *There is reward for your accomplishment, says Hashem . . .
and your children will return to their own border* (ibid. 31:15,16).

50:13 His[13] sons carried him to Canaan, and they buried
him in the Cave of the Machpelah Field, bordering
**Mamrei. [This is] the field that Avraham bought as burial
property from Efron, the Hittite.**

HIS SONS CARRIED HIM—but not his grandsons, for he had commanded them, "Neither an Egyptian nor any of your sons who are
born of Canaanite daughters shall carry my coffin. Only you [my
children, shall carry me.]"

He assigned positions for them [around the coffin]: Three [car-
rying the coffin] on the east, and the same for all four directions.
He arranged them in the same order as they would be arranged in
the desert [around the Mishkan.] Levi did not carry [the coffin,]
for [his tribe] was destined to carry the Ark, and Yosef did not carry
[the coffin] for he was a king. Menasheh and Efraim took their
places. This is the meaning of, *The Children of Yisrael shall encamp,
each man by his banner according to the sign of their fathers*
(*Bamidbar* 2:2)—according to the sign their father [Yaakov] had
given them when carrying his coffin.

---

13 Yaakov's sons.

שמות

SHEMOS

———◉———

1:1 These are the names of the children of Yisrael who came to Egypt with Yaakov; each with his family.

THESE ARE THE NAMES OF THE CHILDREN OF YISRAEL—Although [G-d] counted them by name in their lifetime (*Bereishis* 46:8-27), He counted them again after their death; letting us know how dearly He loved them. They are compared to the stars which He takes out at night [from their heavenly abode] and brings in [in the morning] by number and name, as it says, *Who takes out their hosts by number, calling all of them by name* (*Yeshayah* 40:26).

1:12 But as much as [the Egyptians] will oppress [the children of Yisrael], so will they increase and gain strength. [The Egyptians] were disgusted because of the children of Yisrael.

BUT AS MUCH AS [THE EGYPTIANS] WILL OPPRESS THEM—As much as [the Egyptians] set their heart to afflict them, so did the Holy One, blessed be He, set his heart to increase and strengthen them. ["Will oppress them," in future tense suggests that the moment the Egyptians thought of oppressing the Jews, G-d had increased and strengthened them.]

THE BIRTH OF MOSHE

2:1 [Amram], a man of the house of Levi went and married [Yocheved], a daughter of Levi.

MARRIED [YOCHEVED], A DAUGHTER OF LEVI—Because of Pharaoh's decree [that *every boy who is born must be cast into the Nile* (1:12)], he separated from her [so he would not beget children.] Now he took [Yocheved] back, marrying her a second time. She too, was transformed, becoming like a young woman, although she was 130 years old [at the time. Proof that this is so:] She was born between the walls [on the border] when [B'nei Yisrael] arrived in Egypt. B'nei Yisrael stayed in Egypt for 210 years, and when they left Egypt, Moshe was 80 years old. Therefore, when she conceived [Moshe] she must have been 130 years old, [yet the Torah] calls her *a daughter of Levi*, [a term befitting a young woman].

2:2 The woman became pregnant and gave birth to a son. When she saw that he was good she hid him for three months.

HE WAS GOOD—When he was born the entire house filled with light. ["Goodness" is equated with "light," as in, *G-d saw that the light was good* (*Bereishis* 1:3)]

2:3 When she could no longer hide him, she took for him a reed basket, smearing it with clay and tar. She placed the child in it, and put it in the bulrushes at the bank of the Nile.

SMEARING IT WITH CLAY AND TAR—Tar on the outside and clay on the inside, so the *tzaddik* [Moshe] should not smell the offensive odor of tar.

2:7 The [infant's] sister said to Pharaoh's daughter, "Shall I go and call for you a Hebrew woman to nurse the child for you?"

A HEBREW WOMAN—This teaches us that Pharaoh's daughter took him to many Egyptian women, but Moshe would not nurse from them because [Egyptian women eat unclean food, and he did not want to defile his mouth which] was destined to speak with the *Shechinah*.

2:11 It happened in those days. Moshe had grown and went out to his people and saw their hard labor. He saw an Egyptian beating one of his fellow Hebrews.

HE SAW THEIR HARD LABOR—He directed his eyes and heart to be distressed over them. [He did not merely look at them as a neutral observer but was deeply touched by their plight.]

2:13 Moshe went out the next day, and saw two Hebrew men fighting. "Why do you want to strike your brother?" he demanded of the wicked one.

WHY DO YOU WANT TO STRIKE YOUR BROTHER?—He is called *the wicked one* for merely raising his hand, even though he did not actually strike him.

2:14 "Who made you our prince and judge?" retorted [the other]? "Do you mean to say you will kill me as you killed the Egyptian?" Moshe was frightened, and said, "The matter is known."

DO YOU MEAN TO SAY YOU WILL KILL ME?—From [the words "to say you will kill"] we learn that [Moshe] killed [the Egyptian by uttering] G-d's ineffable Name.

MOSHE WAS FRIGHTENED—According to its plain meaning, [Moshe was afraid that Pharaoh would kill him for slaying the Egyptian.] The Midrash explains [that Moshe] worried because he saw wicked men and informers among Yisrael. He thought, "Since this is so, perhaps [the Jews] do not deserve to be redeemed [from bondage].

"THE MATTER IS KNOWN," HE SAID—According to its plain meaning, [it is known that he had slain the Egyptian]. The Midrash explains it as follows: [Moshe said,] Now I understand. I used to wonder: In what way did Yisrael sin more than all the seventy nations of the world that they should be punished with harsh labor? Now I see that they deserve it.

2:20 [Yisro] asked his daughters, "Where is he now? Why did you leave the man behind? Call him, that he may eat bread [with us]."

WHY DID YOU LEAVE THE MAN BEHIND?—[Yisro] recognized that [Moshe] was a descendant of Yaakov, for [his daughters told him that] the water [of the well] rose toward him [as it did for Yaakov at the well in Charan].

HASHEM REVEALS HIMSELF TO MOSHE ASKING HIM TO LEAD YISRAEL FROM EGYPT

3:2 The angel of Hashem appeared to [Moshe] in a flame of fire out of the midst of a thorn-bush. As he looked, [Moshe] realized that the bush was on fire but was not being consumed.

THE ANGEL APPEARED . . . OUT OF THE MIDST OF A THORN-BUSH— But not out of the midst of any other tree. [By appearing in a thorn-bush whose thorns sting and cause pain, G-d demonstrated that He shares in the agony of the Jewish people,] as it says, *I am with you in distress* (*Tehillim* 91:15).

3:11 Moshe said to G-d, "Who am I that I should go to Pharaoh? And [who am I] that I should bring the children of Yisrael out of Egypt?"

WHO AM I?—Of what importance am I that I should speak with kings?

AND [WHO AM I] THAT I SHOULD BRING THE CHILDREN OF YISRAEL OUT OF EGYPT?—And even if I am important, what merit does Yisrael have that a miracle be performed for them, and that I take them out of Egypt?

3:12 And He said, "For I will be with you, and this is the sign for you that it was I who sent you: When you will bring the people out of Egypt, you will [all] serve G-d on this mountain."

AND HE SAID, "FOR I SHALL BE WITH YOU"—[G-d] first answered Moshe's first question, and then his second [question. G-d said, regarding your question,] *Who am I that I should go to Pharaoh?* This [mission] is not yours but Mine, *For I will be with you.* [You are not petitioning Pharaoh on your own behalf, but on Mine, and you will tell him that I sent you.] *And this*—the vision that you have seen at the thorn-bush—*is the sign for you that it was I who sent you*, and that you will succeed in My mission, and that I am able to save you. Just as you saw the thorn-bush carry out My mission [of burning without being consumed,] so too, you will carry out my mission without being harmed.

As for your question: What merit does Yisrael have that they should depart from Egypt? I have a momentous matter [in whose merit] they will leave Egypt. Three months after departing Egypt they are destined to receive the Torah on this mountain.

FOR I WILL BE WITH YOU. AND THIS IS THE SIGN FOR YOU THAT IT WAS I WHO SENT YOU. Another explanation:—the fact that you will be successful in this mission, *is the sign for you* of [the fulfillment of] another promise, for I promise you that when you take them out of Egypt, *you will [all]serve G-d on this mountain,* by receiving My Torah on it. This merit will stand Yisrael in good stead [making them worthy of being redeemed from Egypt.]

Similarly [a predicted event served as a portent for the fulfillment of another event in the more distant future, is found] in the verse, *This is a sign for you that this year you will be eating wild growth* (*Yeshayah* 37:30). The prophet foretells that the downfall of Sancheriv will be a sign for the fulfillment of another promise, stating that [although today] your land is barren of fruit, I will bless the things that grow by themselves [and you will have an abundance of food].

3:14 G-d said to Moshe, "I Will Be, Who I Will Be." [G-d then explained,] "This is what you must say to the children of Yisrael, '*I Will Be* sent me to you.'"

I WILL BE WHO I WILL BE—"I will be with them" in the present trouble, "as I will be with them" when they are subjugated by other kingdoms. Whereupon Moshe said to Him, "Master of the universe! Why should I mention other troubles to them? They have enough with the present trouble." [G-d] replied, "You have spoken well. Say, "*I Will Be* sent me to you."

3:15 G-d then said to Moshe, "You must say to the children of Yisrael, 'Hashem, the G-d of your fathers, the G-d of Avraham, the G-d of Yitzchak, and the G-d of Yaakov has sent me to you.' This is My name forever, and this is how I am to be recalled for all generations."

THIS IS MY NAME FOREVER—[The Hebrew word for forever is *le'olam,* however here it] is written without a *vav* and therefore can be read as *le'aleim,* [which means] "to be hidden," teaching that we must not pronounce G-d's name the way it is written [Y-H-V-H.]

AND THIS IS HOW I AM TO BE RECALLED—[G-d] taught [Moshe] that [His name] should be pronounced [as *Ad-onai*, "my L-rd".] David also said, *Hashem, Your name is eternal; the mention of Your name [Ad-onai] is for every generation* (*Tehillim* 135:14).

4:2 G-d asked, "What is this in your hand?" And [Moshe] replied, "A staff."

"WHAT IS THIS IN YOUR HAND?"—[In Hebrew "What is this" is usually written as two words: *mah zeh*.] Here it is written as one word *mazeh*, [which translates as "from this"] to be expounded as follows: With this [staff that you are holding] in your hand, you deserve to be beaten, for you have suspected innocent people, [saying, *They will not believe me* (4:1)].

4:3 [G-d] said, "Throw it[14] to the ground!" When Moshe threw it on the ground, it turned into a snake, and Moshe ran away from it.

IT TURNED INTO A SNAKE—[By turning the staff into a snake] G-d hinted to [Moshe] that he had slandered Yisrael when he said, *They will not believe me* (4:1). He thereby adopted the strategy of the snake [who enticed Chavah to eat the forbidden fruit by slandering G-d. He said G-d created the world by eating from the tree.][15]

4:6 Hashem [then] said to Moshe, "Place your hand in your chest." Moshe placed his hand in his chest, he then removed it and behold it was leprous, [as white] as snow.

IT WAS LEPROUS, [AS WHITE] AS SNOW—*Tzaraas* [leprosy] presents as white, as it says, *If it is a white baheres-mark*[16] (*Vayikra* 13:4). With this sign, too, G-d hinted to Moshe that he had maligned

---

14 The staff.
15 Rashi on *Bereishis* 3:5.
16 *baheres* is a form of *tzaraas* (leprosy).

[Yisrael] when he said, "*They will not believe me.*" He punished Moshe with *tzaraas*, just as Miriam was stricken with *tzaraas* for maligning [Moshe] (*Bamidbar* 12:1-13).

4:8 [Hashem said,] "If they do not believe you, and they do not pay attention to the first miraculous sign, then they will believe the evidence of the second sign."

THEN THEY WILL BELIEVE THE EVIDENCE OF THE SECOND SIGN— When you tell them, "I was stricken because I spoke disparagingly about you," they will believe you, for they have already learned that those who harm them are stricken with plagues, such as Pharaoh and Avimelech [who were afflicted with *tzaraas* when they abducted] Sarah.

4:10 Moshe pleaded with Hashem, "I beg you, O Hashem. I am not a man of words—not since yesterday, not since the day before—not since the very first time You spoke to me, for heavy of tongue and heavy of mouth am I."

NOT SINCE YESTERDAY—[These words] teach us that the Holy One, blessed be He, spent seven full days at the thorn-bush prevailing upon Moshe to undertake His mission. The phrase, *not since yesterday, not since the day before—not since the very first time You spoke to me*, denotes three days, and the word *gam*, mentioned three times, implies the inclusion of [three] additional days, bringing us to six days. Additionally Moshe stood [before G-d] saying, "*Send whomever you wish to send [just not me]*" (4:13), [continuing to hesitate] until G-d became angry [and Moshe] agreed to undertake [the mission]. Moshe was reluctant, unwilling to outrank his brother Aharon who was both older and a prophet, as it says in reference to Aharon, *Did I not reveal Myself to your father's house in Egypt?* (1 *Shemuel* 2:27). In the same vein, it says, *I made Myself known to them in the land of Egypt, and I said to them, "Each man should cast away his detestable idols"* (*Yechezkel* 20:5-7), and this prophecy was said to Aharon [before Moshe's vision at the thorn-bush].

4:14 Hashem displayed anger at Moshe and He said, "Is not Aharon the Levite your brother? I know that *he* knows how to speak! He is setting out to meet you, and when he sees you, his heart will be glad."

WHEN HE SEES YOU, HIS HEART WILL BE GLAD—Not as you think that he will resent you because you are outranking him. Because of [his humility and good-heartedness] Aharon merited [to wear] the ornament of the Kohen Gadol's breastplate which was placed over his heart.

4:20 Moshe took his wife and sons, and putting them on the donkey, set out to return to Egypt. He took the divine staff in his hand.

PUTTING THEM ON THE DONKEY—[It does not say "on a donkey," rather, "on the donkey."] This was the donkey that Avraham had saddled for the binding of Yitzchak. It is [the same donkey on which] the King Mashiach [will ride] when he is revealed to us, as it says, *[Mashiach will appear as] a humble man riding on a donkey* (*Zechariah* 9:9).

4:23 I [G-d] have told you [Pharaoh] to let My son go and serve Me. If you refuse to let him leave, I will kill your first-born son.

I WILL KILL YOUR FIRST-BORN SON—Though this is the last [of the ten plagues], He warned Pharaoh about it first, because it was the most severe of all plagues, [and He hoped to frighten Pharaoh into letting Yisrael go]. And so it says, *Behold! G-d is beyond reach in His power,* therefore, *Who can give guidance as He does?* (*Iyov* 36:22) [G-d reveals His plans before carrying them out, whereas,] a man of flesh and blood who seeks vengeance from his fellow, hides his plans so [the intended victim] should not escape [from his wrath]. The Holy One, blessed be He, is powerful beyond reach, and no one can escape from Him, except by doing *teshuvah*. Therefore, He shows [the sinner the punishment that awaits him,] warning him to repent.

5:1 Moshe and Aharon then went to Pharaoh and said, "So said Hashem, the G-d of Yisrael, 'Let My people leave, so they can sacrifice for Me in the desert.'"

MOSHE AND AHARON THEN WENT TO PHARAOH—But the elders, [whom Moshe and Aharon had gathered (4:29)], slipped away one by one instead of following Moshe and Aharon. By the time [Moshe and Aharon] arrived at [Pharaoh's] palace, all of them had sneaked away, because they were afraid to go. At Sinai they were paid back, as it says, *Only Moshe shall approach G-d, but they may not come close* (24:2). [The elders wanted to approach Mt. Sinai,] but they were sent back.

5:14 The Jewish foremen, whom Pharaoh's administrators had appointed, were beaten. They were told, "Why didn't you complete your quota to make bricks as the day before yesterday, neither yesterday nor today?"

THE JEWISH FOREMEN . . . WERE BEATEN—The Jewish foremen had pity on their fellows, not forcing them [to produce more bricks]. The foremen, whose job it was to deliver the bricks to the Egyptian taskmasters, were beaten for not pressuring the [Jewish] workers when there was a shortage [in the quota.] Therefore, these foremen merited to become the Sanhedrin, and some of the [divine] spirit that rested on Moshe was placed on them, as it says, *Gather to Me seventy men of the elders of Yisrael* (*Bamidbar* 11:16), those who did good things in Egypt, *for they are the elders of the people and its foremen* (ibid.).

6:1 Hashem said to Moshe, "Now you will see what I will do to Pharaoh, for through a strong hand he will send them out, and through a strong hand he will drive them out of his land."

NOW YOU WILL SEE—You have questioned the way I run the world. You were not like Avraham to whom I first said, "*It is through Yitzchak that you will gain posterity*" (*Bereishis* 21:12), and then said, "*Bring him up there for a burnt offering*" (ibid. 22:2), yet he did not question My ways. Since [you harbor doubt] *now you will see*—you will only see what is happening to Pharaoh, but you will not merit to see what will happen to the seven nations [of Canaan] when I bring [Yisrael] to the land [of Yisrael].

ואֵרָא

VA'EIRA

———◆———

6:2 G-d spoke to Moshe and said to him, "I am Hashem."

G-D SPOKE TO MOSHE—He reproved Moshe because he spoke harshly, saying, "*Why have You harmed this people?*" (*Shemos* 5:22).

AND HE SAID TO HIM, "I AM HASHEM"—[The name Hashem implies] I am faithful to pay a good reward to those who walk before Me. [G-d said, "Moshe, you asked Me, *Why did You send me?*] I have not sent you [to Pharaoh] for nothing, [I sent you] to fulfill the promise I made to the early Fathers."

The phrase, *I am Hashem* when stated in connection with punishment, is interpreted to mean, "I am faithful to exact retribution." For example, *Do not swear falsely by My name, [if you do,] you will be desecrating your G-d's name, I am Hashem* (*Vayikra* 19:12). But when [the phrase *I am Hashem*] is linked to the fulfillment of a commandment, such as, *Be careful regarding My commandments and keep them, I am Hashem* (ibid. 22:31), [it means] "I am faithful to give reward."

6:3 I revealed Myself to Avraham, Yitzchak, and Yaakov [with the name] E-l Shad-dai, but I did not become known to them by My name Hashem.

[WITH THE NAME] E-L SHAD-DAI—Whenever I made promises [to the Fathers], I said to them, "I am E-l Shad-dai."

BUT I DID NOT BECOME KNOWN TO THEM BY MY NAME HASHEM— [The Hebrew for, "I did not become known" is, *lo nodati*.] The verse does not say, *lo hodati*, "I did not mention to them My name Hashem," but *lo nodati*, "I did not become known." This is because [although I mentioned to them My name Hashem,] My attribute of truthfulness was not recognized by them. The name Hashem signifies that I am faithful to keep My word. [I was not known to them by this Name,] because I made promises to them, but have not [yet] kept them.

6:4 I also established My covenant with them, [promising] to give them the land of Canaan, the land where they stayed as foreigners, where they had sojourned.

I ALSO ESTABLISHED MY COVENANT WITH THEM—When I appeared to them as E-l Sha-dai I made a covenant with them.

[PROMISING] TO GIVE THEM THE LAND OF CANAAN—[G-d's promise] to Avraham is in the portion dealing with circumcision, where it says, *I am E-l Shad-dai . . . and I will give you and your off-spring the land where you are now living as a foreigner* (*Bereishis* 17:8). [G-d's promise] to Yitzchak is,] *To you and your offspring I will give all these lands, I will thus keep the oath that I made to your father Avraham* (ibid. 26:3). [Although the promise to Yitzchak does not explicitly state the name E-l Shad-dai, since He promised him the oath he made to Avraham, and] in the oath which He made to Avraham He did use the name E-l Shad-dai. [G-d's promise to] Yaakov was, *I am E-l Shad-dai, be fruitful and increase . . . I will grant you the land that I gave to Avraham and Yitzchak* (*Bereishis* 35:11,12). I made these promises to them but I did not [yet] keep them.

6:13 Hashem spoke to [both] Moshe and Aharon. He instructed them regarding the children of Yisrael and regarding Pharaoh, king of Egypt, to take the children of Yisrael out of Egypt.

HE INSTRUCTED THEM REGARDING THE CHILDREN OF YISRAEL—He instructed [Moshe and Aharon] to lead the children of Yisrael gently, being patient with them [if the Jews spoke harshly to them].

6:23 Aharon married Elisheva, daughter of Aminadav, Nachshon's sister. She bore him, Nadav, Avihu, Elazar and Isamar.

NACHSHON'S SISTER—From here we learn that before one takes a wife he should investigate [the character] of her brothers, [because most children take after the brothers of their mother].

6:26 This is Aharon and Moshe to whom Hashem said, "Bring the children of Yisrael out of Egypt according to their legions."

THIS IS AHARON AND MOSHE TO WHOM HASHEM SAID—Sometimes the Torah places Aharon before Moshe, and other times Moshe is placed before Aharon, to tell us they are equal.

THE PLAGUES OF EGYPT

7:3 I will harden Pharaoh's heart, and I will increase My signs and My wonders in the land of Egypt.

I WILL HARDEN—[Is it fair for G-d to make Pharaoh obstinate, so He can punish him?] Since [Pharaoh] behaved in a wicked fashion, audaciously defying Me, and I know full well that the idolatrous nations have no desire to repent sincerely, it is fair that his heart is hardened, so I can increase My miraculous signs, so [Yisrael] will recognize My power. This is the way the Holy One, blessed be He, acts: He brings punishment on the idolatrous nations so Yisrael will take notice and fear Him, as it says, *I wiped out nations, their towers are desolate; I turned their thoroughfares into ruins, with none passing by . . . I thought that you would fear Me, would learn a lesson* (*Tzefaniah* 3:6,7). Despite this, [G-d did not make Pharaoh obstinate] for the first five plagues as it says, *Pharaoh's heart remained hardened* [without G-d's instigation], rather than *Hashem hardened Pharaoh's heart.*

7:19 Hashem said to Moshe to tell Aharon, "Take your staff and extend your hand over the waters of Egypt—over their rivers, their canals, their ponds, and over all their bodies of water—and [the water] shall turn to blood. There will be blood throughout all Egypt, even in wooden [barrels] and stone [jars]."

TELL AHARON—Since the river protected Moshe when he was cast into it, the plagues of blood and frogs were not struck by him; rather the river was struck by Aharon.

8:18 On that day I will set apart the land of Goshen where My people remain, so that there will not be any harmful creatures there. You will then realize that I am G-d, right here on earth.

YOU WILL THEN REALIZE THAT I AM G-D, RIGHT HERE ON EARTH— Although My abode is in heaven, My decree is upheld even in the lower worlds.

בא

Bo

⟫━━━⟩●⟨━━━⟪

10:22 Moshe lifted his hand toward the sky, and there was an opaque darkness in all of Egypt, lasting for three days.

THERE WAS AN OPAQUE DARKNESS—Why did He bring the plague of darkness on them? Wicked individuals among the Jews of that generation did not wish to leave Egypt. They died during the three days of darkness, so the Egyptians should not see their downfall and say, "They too, are struck [by disaster] just as we are." Furthermore, [during the darkness] the Jews searched and noticed the Egyptians' vessels. Later, when they departed and asked [the Egyptians for vessels,] the Egyptians answered, "We don't have any," and the Jews replied, "I saw it in your house in such and such place."

11:8 [Moshe said to Pharaoh,] "All these officials of yours will come and bow down to me, saying, 'Leave! You and all your followers!' Only then will I leave."

ALL THESE OFFICIALS OF YOURS WILL COME—Out of respect for the king [Moshe did not say that Pharaoh would come.] However, ultimately Pharaoh himself came to Moshe in the night, saying, *"Get moving! Get out from among my people"* (*Shemos* 12:31). Yet Moshe did not tell him at the beginning, "You will come to me, and you will bow down to me."

SACRIFICING THE PASCHAL LAMB

12:1,3 And Hashem Spoke to Moshe and Aharon in the land of Egypt saying. . . . Speak to the entire community of Yisrael, saying, "On the tenth of this month, every man must take a lamb for each extended family, a lamb for each household."

SPEAK TO THE ENTIRE COMMUNITY OF YISRAEL—[The Hebrew word for speak *dabberu* is in the plural, as if G-d were addressing both Moshe and Aharon]. Did Aharon speak [the word of Hashem]? Was it not Moshe who was told, "*You shall speak to the children of Yisrael*" (*ibid.* 31:13)?—However [Moshe and Aharon] accorded honor to each other saying, "Teach me [the law] that G-d has told you." Thus it sounded as if both of them were speaking.

12:6 Hold [the lamb] in safekeeping until the fourteenth day of this month. The entire community of Yisrael shall then slaughter [their sacrifices] in the afternoon.

HOLD [THE LAMB] IN SAFEKEEPING—[This does not mean "prevent it from running away,"] rather, examine it for blemishes four days before its slaughter. Why did G-d require that the [the lamb for the Pesach sacrifice in Egypt] be set aside four days before its slaughter, whereas He did not require this for the Pesach offering of later generations? Rabbi Masya ben Charash answered this question, saying, G-d says, *I passed by you [in Egypt], and I saw you, and behold, your time was the time of love* (*Yechezkel* 16:8). The time has come to fulfill the oath I made to Avraham to redeem his children. But [the children of Yisrael] had no mitzvos to do on that night to merit redemption, as it says, *You were naked and bare* (ibid. 16:7). Therefore He gave them two mitzvos: the blood of the Pesach offering and the blood of circumcision. They circumcised themselves on that night [before eating the Pesach offering,] as it says, *I saw you wallowing in your bloods* (ibid. 16:6)—soiled with the two bloods of [Pesach and *milah*]. G-d said also, *You too, with the blood of your covenant I have freed your prisoners from a pit in which there was no water* (*Zechariah* 9:11) [i.e., neither Torah nor mitzvos which are compared to water]. Since the Jews were enthralled by [Egyptian] idolatry, [which involved the worship of the sheep,] Moshe said to them, *Withdraw and take for yourselves sheep* (*Shemos* 12:21), [meaning,] "Withdraw from the worship [of sheep], and take for yourselves sheep for the mitzvah." [They took the sheep four days before slaughtering it, to internalize that they were offering sheep they had hitherto been worshipping. This was not necessary in later generations.]

12:13 The blood will be a sign for you on the houses where you are staying. I will see the blood and pass you by. There will not be any deadly plague among you when I strike Egypt.

I WILL SEE THE BLOOD—[Why must G-d see the blood? Is not] everything revealed to Him? The Holy One, blessed be He, said, "I will focus My attention, and noticing you engaged in doing the mitzvah [of placing the blood on your doorposts], I will skip over you."

12:28 The children of Yisrael went and did as Hashem had instructed Moshe. They did it exactly.

THE CHILDREN OF YISRAEL WENT AND DID—[The commandment to bring the Pesach sacrifice on the fourteen of Nissan was given two weeks earlier on Rosh Chodesh Nissan. Yet the verse states that immediately following the command they went and did.] Did they bring the Pesach offering at that point in time? Weren't they commanded on Rosh Chodesh, and therefore they did not bring it yet? We see from here, that as soon as they agreed [to do the mitzvah], the Torah credits them with the actual fulfillment.

12:34 The people took their dough before it could rise. Their leftover dough was wrapped in their robes [and placed] on their shoulders.

ON THEIR SHOULDERS—Although they took many animals with them [on which they could have placed the dough, they carried the leftover matzah on their shoulders] to show their love for the mitzvah.

12:39 They baked the dough that they had brought out of Egypt into unleavened [matzah] cakes, since it had not risen. They had been driven out of Egypt and could not delay, and they had not prepared any provisions.

THEY HAD NOT PREPARED ANY PROVISIONS—for the journey. [The Torah] is relating the praise of Yisrael. They did not say, "How can we go into the wilderness without provisions?" Rather, they believed [in G-d's word] and left. The prophet Yirmeyah expresses this, saying, *I remembered for your favor the kindness of your youth, your love as a bride—how you followed Me in the wilderness, in a land not sown* (*Yirmeyah* 2:2). What is [Yisrael's] reward [for this trust?] It is stated explicitly after this: *Yisrael is holy to Hashem, the first fruits of His harvest* (ibid. 2:3).

12:41 At the end of 430 years, on that very day, all of Hashem's legions left Egypt.

ON THAT VERY DAY—As soon as the end of this era arrived, the Omnipresent did not keep [Yisrael] back even for a blink of an eye. The angels came to Avraham on the fifteenth of Nissan [announcing the birth of Yitzchak,] and on the fifteenth of Nissan, Yitzchak was born. [Thirty years earlier,] on the fifteenth of Nissan, the Pact between the Parts [foretelling the Egyptian exile] was made. [And on the fifteenth of Nissan, Yisrael left Egypt].

13:4 You left this day, in the month of spring.

IN THE MONTH OF SPRING—Don't we know in which month they went out? Yet Moshe [mentioned the month of their departure] telling them, "Look how kindly [G-d] treated you, taking you out in a month suited for travel, neither too sunny, nor too cold, and not rainy. The same idea is expressed in, *He takes out prisoners at the most suitable time* (*Tehillim* 68:7), meaning, [He took out the Jews imprisoned in Egypt] in the month that is perfect for departure.

13:16 And [these words] shall be as a sign on your arm and as an emblem in the center of your head.

AND AS AN EMBLEM IN THE CENTER OF YOUR HEAD—[The Hebrew word used for "an emblem" is *totafos*, which] refers to *tefillin*. Since the [head *tefillin*] has four compartments [containing the four *parshiyos*], they are called *totafos,* for *tat* in the Kaspi language means two; and *pas* in the Afriki language means two. [Thus *totafos*—a combination of *tat* and *pas*, equals four.] Menachem [ibn Saruk, the great grammarian] conjugates [*totafos* as an expression of speech, as in, *speak* [vehateif] *to the south* (*Yechezkel* 21:2), and, *do not preach* [al tatifu] (*Michah* 2:6). This interpretation is in line with the description of *[tefillin]* in an earlier verse as *a remembrance between your eyes* (*Shemos* 13:9). For whoever sees the *tefillin* [bound between the eyes] will remember the miracle [of the Exodus] and speak about it.

בשלח

BESHALACH

———◆◆◆———

THE SPLITTING OF THE REED SEA

14:4 I will harden the heart of Pharaoh and he will chase after them. I will be glorified through Pharaoh and his entire army, and Egypt will know that I am Hashem. And they [the Bnei Yisrael] did as they were instructed.

I WILL BE GLORIFIED THROUGH PHARAOH—When the Holy One, blessed be He, takes revenge against the wicked, His name becomes magnified and glorified. Thus it says [in connection with the destruction of Gog], *I will contend with him* (*Yechezkel* 38:22,23), [and in the wake of that,] *I will become magnified, and I will become sanctified, and I will become known.* Similarly, it says [about the defeat of Sancheriv,] *There he broke the flying arrows of the bow* (*Tehillim* 76:4), and as a result, *G-d has become known among Yehudah* (ibid. 78:2). Similarly it says, *Hashem has become known, He has carried out judgment* (ibid.9:17).

THROUGH PHARAOH AND HIS ENTIRE ARMY—[Pharaoh] was the one who launched the sinful [oppression of Yisrael], therefore the punishment started with him.

AND THEY DID AS THEY WERE INSTRUCTED—This verse praises Yisrael. They obeyed Moshe; instead of saying, "How can we draw close to our pursuers? We must run away! They said, "Our only option is to follow the orders of [Moshe] son of Amram."

14:5 **The king of Egypt received the news that the people were escaping. Pharaoh and his officials changed their minds regarding the people and said, "What have we done? How could we have released Yisrael from doing our work?"**

THE KING OF EGYPT RECEIVED THE NEWS—[Pharaoh] sent undercover agents with [Yisrael to ensure that they remained in the desert for only three days to bring sacrifices]. After the three days they were to go and return had passed, the agents realized that they were not returning to Egypt. They informed Pharaoh of this on the fourth day. On the fifth and sixth day the Egyptians chased after Yisrael, and on the night preceding the seventh day they went down into the sea. In the morning [of the seventh day], Yisrael sang the Song of the Sea (*Shemos* 15:1-18). Therefore, we read the Song [of the Sea] on the seventh day [of Pesach].

14:6 **[Pharaoh] harnessed his chariots, and summoned his people to go with him.**

[PHARAOH] HARNESSED HIS CHARIOTS—He himself did this [menial chore, not his servants].

AND SUMMONED HIS PEOPLE TO GO WITH HIM—He swayed them with [fiery] oratory, saying, "We have been battered! They took our money and we sent them away! Come with me and we will go after them! I will not deal with you as other kings do. Other kings have their soldiers go ahead of them in battle but I will go ahead of you!" As it says, *Pharaoh brought himself near* (ibid. 11:10), meaning, he hurried ahead of his army. [Pharaoh continued,] "Other kings take their share of the spoils first, grabbing as much as they want. I will share equally with you," as it says, *I will divide the spoils* (ibid.15:9).

14:7 He took 600 choice chariots, as well as the entire chariot corps of Egypt, with officers over them all.

AS WELL AS THE ENTIRE CHARIOT CORPS OF EGYPT—He took all the remaining chariots, besides [the 600 choice chariots]. Where did he find all the animals [to pull the chariots]? If you say they belonged to the Egyptians, doesn't it say, *All the livestock in Egypt died* (ibid. 9:6)? And if you say they belonged to Yisrael, doesn't it say, *Our livestock must also go along with us* (ibid.10:26)? So whose [animals] were they? They belonged to those [Egyptians] who feared the word of Hashem, [and heeding G-d's warning of the plague of hail, kept their slaves and livestock indoors] (ibid.9:20). In light of this, Rabbi Shimon was wont to say: Kill even the best of the Egyptians; crush the brain of even the best of snakes, [for these "G-d-fearing" Egyptians supplied the horses for the pursuing chariots].

14:10 As Pharaoh came close, the children of Yisrael looked up and saw Egypt marching at their rear. The people became very frightened and the children of Yisrael cried out to Hashem.

AND SAW EGYPT MARCHING AT THEIR REAR—[The verse does not say, "The Egyptians," rather "Egypt" in the singular, denoting that the Egyptians] advanced with one heart, as one man.

Another explanation [for "Egypt" in the singular] is that "Egypt" refers to the guardian angel of Egypt. Yisrael saw the guardian angel of Egypt traveling from heaven to help the Egyptians.

THE CHILDREN OF YISRAEL CRIED OUT TO HASHEM—They used the method of their ancestors, [who prayed when they were in distress]. Regarding Avraham it says, *To the place where he had stood [in prayer]* (*Bereishis* 19:27). Regarding Yitzchak it says, *Yitzchak went out to meditate in the field* (ibid. 24:63). Regarding Yaakov it says, *He implored [G-d] in that place* (ibid.28:11).

14:15 Hashem said to Moshe, "Why are you crying out to Me? Speak to the children of Yisrael and let them start moving."

WHY ARE YOU CRYING OUT TO ME?—[This verse] teaches us that Moshe was standing in prayer. The Holy One, blessed be He, said to him, "This is no time for drawn-out prayer, for Yisrael is in distress."

SPEAK TO THE CHILDREN OF YISRAEL AND LET THEM START MOVING—There is nothing for them to do but travel, for the sea will not stop them. The merit of their forefathers, their own merit, and the faith they had in Me when they came out of Egypt, are sufficient to split the sea for them.

14:19 The angel of G-d who had been traveling in front of the camp of the children of Yisrael moved and went behind them. The pillar of cloud thus moved from in front of them and stood at their rear.

AND STOOD AT THEIR REAR—To separate the camp of Yisrael and the camp of Egypt, [preventing the Egyptians from closing in on Yisrael,] and to block the arrows and catapult stones of the Egyptians. In all other places it says, *the angel of Hashem*, but here it says, *The angel of Elo-him*. [The name] *Elo-him* signifies [G-d's] attribute of Justice, [whereas the name Hashem denotes the divine attribute of Mercy. Why was *the angel of Elo-him* sent on the mission of mercy to save Yisrael?] This teaches that Yisrael was being judged at this moment whether to be saved or destroyed with Egypt.

14:20 [The angel] came between the camp of Egypt and the camp of Yisrael. There was a cloud and darkness, and [the pillar of fire] lit up the night. All that night the camp [of Egypt] did not approach the camp [of Yisrael].

[THE ANGEL] CAME BETWEEN THE CAMP OF EGYPT AND THE CAMP
OF YISRAEL—This may be compared to [a father] walking along the
road with his son in front of him. When bandits tried to kidnap his
son, the father placed his son behind him. When a wolf attacked
behind the father, he placed his son in front of him. When bandits
appeared in front of him and wolves came behind him, he carried
[his son] on his arms, fighting them off. And so it says, *I led Efraim
along; I took them on My arms* (*Hoshea* 11:3).

14:21 Moshe extended his hand over the sea. Hashem
drove back the sea with a powerful east wind, during the entire night, transforming the sea bed into dry land.
The waters divided.

THE WATERS DIVIDED—[The plural "waters"] tells us that all the
[bodies of] water of the world divided at that moment.

14:25 He made the chariot wheels fall off, and they could
drive only with great difficulty. The Egyptians
said, "Let us flee from Yisrael, for Hashem is fighting for them
in Egypt."

HASHEM IS FIGHTING FOR THEM IN EGYPT—. . . Another explanation: [Hashem is fighting] in the land of Egypt, for just as the
Egyptian [forces] were stricken at the sea, so were those remaining
in Egypt stricken.

THE SONG OF THE SEA

15:1 Moshe and the children of Yisrael will then sing this
song to Hashem, and they said, "I will sing to
Hashem for He is exalted, yes exalted; a horse and its rider He
hurled into the sea."

MOSHE AND THE CHILDREN OF YISRAEL WILL THEN SING—Our
Rabbis of blessed memory explain [in the Midrash]: From [the fu-

ture tense of, "will sing"] we have an allusion in the Torah to the
revival of the dead, [for Moshe and the children of Yisrael will sing
at the revival of the dead.]

HE IS EXALTED, YES EXALTED—He is exalted beyond all songs—
and, no matter how much I praise Him, there is still more [praise]
to be added. By contrast, a mortal king is praised for qualities he
does not possess (*Mechilta*).

15:2 My strength and song is G-d, which was my deliver-
ance. This is my G-d and I will enshrine Him; the
G-d of my father, and I will exalt Him.

THIS IS MY G-D, AND I WILL ENSHRINE HIM—He revealed Himself
to them in His glory, and they pointed to Him with their finger,
[declaring, "This is my G-d"]. At the sea, even a maidservant saw
things prophets did not see.

I WILL ENSHRINE HIM—[The Hebrew for "I will enshrine Him" is,
ve'anveihu.] Onkelos translates *ve'anveihu* as, "I will make an
abode for Him." As in, *A tranquil dwelling* [nevei] (*Yeshayah*
33:20), and, *a corral for flocks* [nevei] (ibid.65:10). Another explanation: The term *ve'anveihu* is an expression of beauty [*noi*].
Accordingly, our verse means, "I will tell of His beauty and praise
to all mankind." For example, [when the nations will ask Yisrael,]
"How is your Beloved better than any other beloved?" [Yisrael will
answer,] *My Beloved is clear-skinned and ruddy,* continuing to recite
the rest of the paragraph (*Shir Hashirim* 5:9,10).

THE G-D OF MY FATHER—is this One, and I will exalt Him.

THE G-D OF MY FATHER—I am not the first to recognize His sanctity. Rather His sanctity and G-dliness is embedded in me since the
days of my forefathers.

15:3 Hashem is the Master of war; Hashem is His name.

HASHEM IS HIS NAME—His wars are not fought with weapons, rather, He wages war using His name, as David said [to Goliath before the battle], *You come against me with sword, spear, and javelin, but I come against you in the name of Hashem, Lord of Hosts* (1 *Shemuel* 17:45).

Another explanation for *Hashem is His name*: [The name Hashem signifies G-d's attribute of Mercy]. Even when He is waging war and wreaking vengeance on His enemies, His attribute of Mercy sustains the world's population. This is not the way of earthly kings. When an earthly king fights a war he sets aside all his affairs [of state,] unable to both [conduct the war and take care of domestic issues].

15:6 Your right hand, O Hashem, is awesome in power; Your right hand, O Hashem, crushes the foe.

YOUR RIGHT HAND . . . YOUR RIGHT HAND—["Your right hand" is repeated, to tell us that] when Yisrael does the will of G-d, the left hand [which denotes strict justice] becomes like the right hand [which represents mercy.] Therefore the verse is to be understood: *Your right hand is awesome in power*—to save Yisrael, and Your other right hand [i.e., the left hand that usually represents justice which has turned into a right hand] crushes the foe (Mechilta).

However it seems to me, [that the verse is referring to one hand only,] and the right hand [itself] crushes the foe—one hand performing two tasks—which is impossible for man to do.

15:7 In Your great majesty You break Your opponents. You sent forth Your wrath, it devoured them like straw.

YOU BREAK YOUR OPPONENTS—You always break those who rise up against You. And who are those who rise up against You? Those who rise up against Yisrael, as it says, *For behold, Your enemies rage*; and what is this raging? *They plot shrewdly against Your people* (*Tehillim* 83:3,4). Because [they plot against Yisrael] the verse calls them the enemies of the Omnipresent.

15:11 Who is like You among powers, Hashem? Who is like You, majestic in holiness? Awesome in praise, doing wonders.

AWESOME IN PRAISE—[People are] afraid to tell Your praises, fearing that [their praises] may be insufficient, as it says, *To You, silence is praise* (*Tehillim* 65:2). [G-d cannot be praised enough, and praising Him with faint praise is an insult].

15:12 You tilted Your right hand, the earth swallowed them.

YOU TILTED YOUR RIGHT HAND—Since all are placed in the Holy One, blessed be He's hand, when He tilts His right hand, the wicked fall and perish. Thus it says, *When Hashem tilts His hand, the helper will stumble and the one being helped will fall* (*Yeshayah* 31:3). This may be compared to glass vessels held in a person's hand. If he tilts his hand slightly, they fall and break.

15:14 Nations heard and shuddered; terror gripped those who lived in Pelishtim.

TERROR GRIPPED THOSE WHO LIVED IN PELISHTIM—Because they had killed Efraim's descendants who left [the Egyptian exile] prematurely, and left Egypt forcibly, as it says, *The men of [the Pelishtim town of] Gas killed [the sons of Efraim]* (1 *Divrei Hayamim* 7:21).

15:15 Edom's chiefs then panicked; Moav's heroes were seized with trembling. Canaan's residents melted away.

THE CHIEFS OF EDOM PANICKED, THE HEROES OF MOAV WERE SEIZED WITH TREMBLING—Actually they had nothing to fear, since [Yisrael] was not crossing into their territory. However, [they trembled] out of anguish and distress over the glory Yisrael [had attained].

15:16 Fear and dread shall fall upon them; at the greatness of Your arm they will be still as stone. Until Your people crossed, O Hashem. Until the people You acquired crossed over.

THE PEOPLE YOU ACQUIRED—[Since G-d owns the entire world, why mention that He acquired Yisrael?] "You acquired" implies "You loved," [for He loved Yisrael] more than any nation. ["You acquired" is used to mean "You loved"] just as an object which is acquired for a high price is cherished by the one who bought it.

15:17,18 O bring them and plant them on the mount of Your heritage, directed toward the place of Your dwelling which you have made. A Sanctuary, O L-rd, which Your hands established. Hashem will reign forever and ever.

DIRECTED TOWARD THE PLACE YOU DWELL IN—The Beis Hamikdash on earth is situated directly opposite the heavenly Throne, which You made.

A SANCTUARY—Hashem cherishes the *Beis Hamikdash*, for He created the world with one hand, as it says, *My hand founded the earth* (*Yeshayah* 48:13), but will create the Beis Hamikdash with two hands [as it says in our verse *Your hands* (in the plural) *established*]. When will it be built with [G-d's] two hands? When *Hashem will reign forever and ever*, [referring to the] time to come, when He will be King of the entire world.

15:20 Miriam the prophetess, Aharon's sister, took the drum in her hands, and all the women followed her with drums and dancing.

WITH DRUMS AND DANCING—the righteous women of that generation, confident that the Holy One, blessed be He, would perform
miracles for them, took drums out of Egypt with them [to cele-
brate the miracles that would occur].

15:22 Moshe forced Yisrael away from the Red Sea. They
traveled for three days in the Shur Desert without
finding any water.

MOSHE FORCED YISRAEL AWAY—He led them away against their
will, for the Egyptians had adorned their horses with ornaments of
gold, silver, and precious stones, and Yisrael, finding them at the
sea, [did not want to move on.] The spoils taken from the
Egyptians at the sea were greater than the spoils taken from Egypt,
as it says, *We will make you wreaths of gold with spangles of silver*[17]
(*Shir Hashirim* 1:11). Therefore, [Moshe] had to lead them
against their will.

15:26 He said, "If you will listen diligently to Hashem,
your G-d, and do what is upright in His eyes, and
you will give ear to all His commandments and keep all His
decrees, then I will not strike you with any of the sicknesses I
brought on Egypt. For I am Hashem who heals you.

IF YOU WILL LISTEN DILIGENTLY—They must accept [the law] on
themselves.

AND LEND AN EAR TO ALL HIS DECREES—Bend your ears to be
exact in fulfilling [the mitzvos].

ALL HIS DECREES—Things that are the decree of the King, without
any rationale. The evil impulse criticizes [these decrees], [saying],

---

17 The Medrash expounds: The wreaths of gold refers to the spoils of the sea,
which were more valuable than the spangles of silver which refers to the spoils taken
from Egypt.

"What is the sense of forbidding these things? Why were they prohibited?" Examples include, the prohibition of wearing a mixture of wool and linen, the prohibition of eating pork, and [the ritual] of the Red Cow, etc.

I WILL NOT STRIKE YOU WITH ANY OF THE SICKNESSES I BROUGHT ON EGYPT, FOR I AM HASHEM WHO HEALS YOU,—I teach you the Torah and mitzvos so you may be saved from the [sickness I bring on Egypt]. This is like a doctor who says to a person, "Do not eat this thing so you will not contract that sickness." And so it says, *It [obedience to mitzvos] will bring healing to your body* (*Mishlei* 3:8).

THE MANNA, BREAD FROM HEAVEN

16:1 They moved on from Elim, and the entire community of Yisrael came to the Sin Desert. It was the fifteenth of the second month after they had left Egypt.

IT WAS THE FIFTEENTH OF THE SECOND MONTH—The day of this encampment is specifically mentioned, because on that day the cakes they had taken out of Egypt ran out, and they needed manna. We learn from here that they ate sixty-one meals from the leftover dough [through the 15th of Iyar],[18] and the manna descended for them on the 16th of Iyar, which was a Sunday, as is cited in *meseches Shabbos* (87b,88a).

16:5 On the sixth day they will have to prepare what they bring home. It will be twice as much as they gather every other day.

---

18 From the 15th of Nissan to the 15th of Iyar there are actually 31 days, which would require 62 meals [at two meals per day]. However, the meal of the night of the 15th of Nissan [i.e., the night of the Exodus] they ate in Egypt, and it is therefore not included (*Sifsei Chachamim*).

TWICE AS MUCH—[They will gather twice as much] as they gather on the other days of the week. I believe, *what they will bring home, and it will be twice as much,* means: that after bringing home and measuring [the regular portion of manna], they will find [it increased to] twice as much as what they gathered and measured every day. This is also the meaning of, *They gathered double bread* (16:22). [Only] after gathering it, did they find it to be a double portion of bread. The meaning of, *that is why He gives on the sixth day bread for two days* (16:29), is in like vein: He gives you a blessing in your house, to fill the *omer* twice, to have bread for two days.

16:7 In the morning you will see the glory of Hashem. He has heard your complaints which are against Hashem. After all, what are we that you should make [the people] complain against us.

IN THE MORNING YOU WILL SEE—This does not refer to the glory mentioned in the verse, *Hashem's glory was visible in the clouds* (16:10). Rather, [Moshe] said to them: In the evening you will know He has the power to satisfy your craving; [however,] He will not give [you meat], with pleasure and a bright countenance, because you asked for it improperly, on a full stomach. But because you asked for the bread when you needed it, it will come down in the morning with the glory of His radiant countenance. He will bring it down to you lovingly, in the morning, when there is enough time to prepare it, with dew over and under it, as if it were placed in a box.

16:8 Moshe said, "In the evening, Hashem will give you meat to eat, and in the morning there will be enough meat to fill you up. Hashem has heard your complaints which you are actually addressing to Him. What are we? Your complaints are not against us but against Hashem."

HASHEM WILL GIVE YOU MEAT TO EAT—But it does not say, "To fill you up," [as it says regarding bread]. The Torah is teaching a rule of proper conduct, that meat should not be eaten to one's fill.

Why did He bring down the bread in the morning and the meat in the evening? It was appropriate to ask for the bread, because one cannot exist without bread, but they requested the meat improperly, for they had many animals [which they could have slaughtered, instead of complaining they had no meat]. Furthermore, it is possible to exist without meat. Therefore, He gave them [the meat] at a difficult time, at an inconvenient hour [when it would be troublesome to prepare].

16:13 That evening a flock of quail came and covered the camp. Then in the morning there was a layer of dew around the camp.

THERE WAS A LAYER OF DEW AROUND THE CAMP—The dew covered the manna. But elsewhere it says, *When the dew would descend on the camp at night, the manna would descend on it* (11:9) [thus, the manna covered the dew! The inconsistency can be explained as follows:] First, the dew descended on the earth, then the manna descended on the dew, then another layer of dew descended on the manna, so it appeared as if the manna were stored in a box.

16:17 The children of Yisrael went to do this; some gathered more, some less.

SOME GATHERED MORE, SOME LESS—Some took too much and some took too little, but when they came home, each person measured what he had gathered against an *omer*. They found that the one who gathered more did not have more than one *omer* per person in his tent, and the one who gathered less did not have less than one *omer* per person. This was a great miracle.

16:21 [The people] gathered it each morning, according to what each person would eat. Then, when the sun became hot, it melted.

WHEN THE SUN BECAME HOT IT MELTED—The [manna] left in the fields melted and flowed into streams. Gazelles and deer drank from it, and non-Jewish people of the world, who trapped them, thereby tasted the taste of manna, and realized how praiseworthy Yisrael was.

16:22 When Friday came, what they gathered turned out to be a double portion of bread, two *omers* for each person. All the leaders of the community came and reported it to Moshe.

WHAT THEY GATHERED TURNED OUT TO BE *LECHEM MISHNEH*—A DOUBLE PORTION OF BREAD—When they measured what they had gathered, they found double, *lechem mishneh*, two *omers* for each person. The Midrash, however, explains it as [if it read], *lechem meshuneh*, "unusual bread." That day [in honor of Shabbos the manna] changed for the better in its aroma and taste.

16:25 Moshe announced, "Eat it today, for today is Shabbos for Hashem. Today you will not find it in the field."

MOSHE ANNOUNCED, "EAT IT TODAY,"—[Shabbos] in the morning, when they usually gathered [the manna], they asked [Moshe], "Shall we go out [and gather it today] or not?" Moshe told them, "Eat what you already have in your house." In the evening they asked him again whether they should go out [and gather manna]. He replied, "*Today is Shabbos,*" [and you should not go out and gather.] Moshe understanding their worry and fear that perhaps the manna had stopped and would no longer come down, said to them, "*Today you will not find [anything] in the field.*" Why did he add the word *Today*? [He implied,] "Today you will not find [manna], but tomorrow you will find it."

16:29 See that Hashem has given you the Shabbos, therefore He gave you bread for two days on Friday. [On Shabbos] everyone must remain in his place. One may not leave his place [to gather food] on Shabbos.

SEE—with your eyes that Hashem in His glory warns you about the Shabbos, for a miracle is performed every Shabbos eve to give you bread for two days.

16:32 Moshe said, "This is what Hashem has command-ed, 'Fill an *omer* measure with [manna] as a keep-sake for your descendants. They will then see the bread that I fed you in the desert when I brought you out of Egypt.'"

FOR YOUR DESCENDANTS—In the days of Yirmeyah, Yirmeyah ad-monished [the nation], saying, "Why don't you engage in the study of Torah?" They answered, "If we quit working and engage in Torah study, how will we support ourselves?" He took out the jar of manna and said to them, *See the word of Hashem* (*Yirmeyah* 2:31) He did not say "*Hear the word of Hashem*," but rather, "*See the word of Hashem*" [for he showed them the jar of manna. Yirmeyah continued,] "With this [manna] your ancestors were sus-tained. The Omnipresent has many agents to prepare food for those who are in awe of Him."

17:8 Amalek came and attacked Yisrael in Refidim.

AMALEK CAME—This section is placed next to the preceding verse, [*Is Hashem with us or not?*], to say, "I [Hashem] am always with you, ready [to fill] your needs, and yet you say, *Is Hashem with us or not?* I swear by your lives, that the dog [Amalek] will come to bite you, and you will cry out to Me, then you will know where I am." This may be compared to a man who carried his son on his shoulder, taking him on a trip. Whenever the son saw something [he wanted,] he said, "Father, please pick this up and give it to me," and the father gave it to him. This happened time and again, [with the father giving his son whatever he wanted.] Then they met a stranger whom the son asked, "Have you seen my father?" Said the father to [his son], "Don't you know where I am?" [Angrily, the father] threw him down, and a dog came and bit him.

17:9 Moshe said to Yehoshua, "Choose men for us, and go out to battle against Amalek. Tomorrow I will stand on top of the hill with the staff of G-d in my hand."

CHOOSE MEN FOR US—For me and for you. [Moshe thus] equated [Yehoshua] with himself. From here the Sages derived the saying, "Your student's honor should be as dear to you as your own honor (*Avos* 4:12)." From where do we know one should honor his colleague as he reveres his master? From the verse, *Aharon said to Moshe, "I beseech you, my master" (Bamidbar* 12:1). Aharon was older than Moshe, yet he considered him as his master. And how do we know one must revere his teacher as he reveres Heaven? Because [regarding *Eldad and Meidad*] it says, "*My master Moshe, stop them,* they deserve to be destroyed, because they are rebelling against you, and those who rebel against you are considered as if they rebelled against the Holy One, blessed be He."

17:11 As long as Moshe held his hands up, Yisrael would win, but as soon as he let his hands down, the battle would go in Amalek's favor.

AS LONG AS MOSHE HELD HIS HANDS UP—Would the hands of Moshe win the war? The Gemara in *Rosh Hashanah* 29a answers this question, [as follows: As long as Yisrael looked toward heaven subjecting their hearts to their Father in Heaven they prevailed, but when they did not, they fell.]

17:12 When Moshe's hands became weary, they took a stone and placed it under him, and he sat on it.

WHEN MOSHE'S HANDS BECAME WEARY—Because he was lax in the performance of the mitzvah, appointing someone else [to command Yisrael's forces in battle rather than leading them] himself, his hands grew weary.

THEY TOOK A STONE AND PLACED IT UNDER HIM—Moshe did not sit on a pillow or cushion, because he said, "Yisrael is enduring pain, let me share their pain."

17:16 He said, "The hand is on *Keis Kah*—G-d's Throne. Hashem shall be at war with Amalek for all generations."

THE HAND IS ON *KEIS KAH*—G-D'S THRONE—The hand of the Holy One, blessed be He, is raised to swear by His Throne that He will forever be at war and harbor enmity against Amalek. Why is the word *kisei*—throne—shortened and spelled *keis*? And why is the Divine Name divided in half [using the Two-Letter Name of Y-H, instead of the Four-Letter name of Y-H-V-H]?—The Holy One, blessed be He, swore that His Name is not whole, nor is His throne whole until the name of Amalek is completely erased. When [Amalek's] name is wiped out completely, the [divine] Name will be whole, and the Throne will be whole, as it says, *O enemy! Your destruction will last forever* (*Tehillim* 9:7), which refers to Amalek about whom it says, *His fury is kept eternally* (*Amos* 1:11), and, *You have torn down their cities, their [i.e., Amalek's] remembrance is lost* (*Tehillim* 9:6). What does the next verse say? *Hashem* [using the full name of Hashem] *will abide eternally* (ibid. 9:8), thus showing that after the annihilation of Amalek, the Name is complete. The verse continues, *He readies His kisei—Throne—for judgment* (ibid. 9:8); thus the Throne is complete.

יתרו
YISRO

—◦◉◦—

18:5 Yisro, the father-in-law of Moshe, came together with [Moshe's] wife and sons to the desert, where Moshe was staying near the mountain of G-d.

TO THE DESERT—We know full well that they were in the desert. [Why must the Torah mention it?] The Torah is praising Yisro; although he held a position of supreme honor, he was impelled to go to the barren desert, to hear Torah teachings.

18:11 Now I know that G-d is the greatest of all the gods, because the very thing that they intentionally sinned came on them.

BECAUSE THE VERY THING THEY INTENTIONALLY SINNED CAME ON THEM—Understand this as the Targum interprets it: [The Egyptians] planned to destroy [Yisrael by drowning their children in the Nile] with water, so they themselves were destroyed with water [by being drowned in the Red Sea].

THAT THEY INTENTIONALLY SINNED—[The Hebrew for "they intentionally sinned" is, *zadu*, which,] means they acted wickedly. Our Rabbis interpret the word *zadu* as [a cognate of cooking] as in the verse, *Yaakov cooked [vayazed] a stew (Bereishis 25:29)*. In other words: In the very pot in which they [were preparing to cook Yisrael], they themselves were cooked.

18:12 **Yisro brought burnt offerings and [other] sacrifices to G-d. Aharon and all the elders of Yisrael came to share the meal with Moshe's father-in-law before G-d.**

BEFORE G-D—From here we learn that if one attends a meal at which Torah scholars are taking part, it is as if he relished the radiance of the *Shechinah* (Divine Presence).

18:13 **The next day, Moshe sat to judge the people. They stood around Moshe from morning to evening.**

THE NEXT DAY, MOSHE SAT TO JUDGE THE PEOPLE. THEY STOOD AROUND MOSHE—He sat like a king, and [those who came to be judged] stood. This annoyed Yisro, for [it appeared as if] Moshe demeaned the honor of Yisrael. Thus, he admonished him, as it says [in the next verse,] *"Why are you sitting by yourself and letting all the people stand around you morning until evening?"* (18:14).

FROM MORNING TO EVENING—Is it possible [that Moshe actually sat and judged all day]? The verse teaches us that if a judge passes judgment with absolute truthfulness even for a single hour, the Torah considers it as if he learned Torah all day, and as if he were a partner of the Holy One, blessed be He, in the creation of the world about which it says, *It was evening and it was morning* (*Bereishis* 1:5).

THE GIVING OF THE TORAH

19:1 **In the third month after the children of Yisrael left Egypt, on this day, they came to the desert of Sinai.**

ON THIS DAY—. . . [Instead of *on this day*, which refers to the present,] it should have said "on that day" [for the verse refers to something that happened in the past]. *On this day* teaches that the words of the Torah should always seem new to you, as if they were given today.

19:2 **They departed from Refidim and arrived at the Sinai Desert, camping in the wilderness. Yisrael camped opposite the mountain.**

YISRAEL CAMPED OPPOSITE THE MOUNTAIN—[The Torah uses the word *vayichan* which is singular and translates as "he camped," instead of *vayachanu*, which means "they camped,"] to demonstrate that they were united in purpose, as one man, with one heart; but at the other encampments there were complaints and discord.

19:4 **You saw what I did to Egypt. I carried you on the wings of eagles and brought you to Me.**

YOU SAW—This is not a tradition handed down to you [by your parents]. Nor am I sending you an oral report, or witnesses to testify to you [about miracles that were performed]. You [with your own eyes] saw what I did to Egypt. [Although the Egyptians] were accountable to Me for many sins even before they attacked you, I only punished them because of [what they did to] you.

ON THE WINGS OF EAGLES—Like an eagle, who carries its fledglings on its wings. All other birds carry their young between their feet, because they are afraid of the birds that fly above them. However, since no bird can fly above the eagle, it is only afraid of man, fearing that he may shoot an arrow at him. He therefore places [his fledglings] on his wings, saying, "Better the arrow should pierce me than my son." [Says G-d,] "I did the same thing," [as it says,] *G-d's angel traveled . . . and came between the camp of Egypt and the camp of Yisrael* (*Shemos* 14:19,20). The Egyptians shot arrows and catapult stones, which the Cloud [of G-d] caught.

19:5 And now if you obey Me and keep My covenant, you shall be My treasure among all people because the entire world is Mine.

AND NOW—If you accept the Torah on yourselves now [when it is difficult for you,] it will become pleasant for you from now on, for all beginnings are difficult.

A TREASURE—[This means] "a cherished treasure," as in, *a treasure of kings* (*Koheles* 2:8), that is, expensive vessels and precious stones which kings store away. So too, will you be a greater treasure to Me than the other nations. Lest you say you are My only possession, without any other [nation] beside you, and therefore my love for you is not treasured, the verse continues, *the entire world is Mine,* yet [the other nations] don't mean anything to Me.

19:8 All the people answered as one and said, "All that Hashem has spoken, we will do." Moshe brought the people's reply back to Hashem.

MOSHE BROUGHT THE PEOPLE'S REPLY BACK TO HASHEM—. . . Was it necessary for Moshe to report the people's answer to G-d? This verse teaches proper conduct through Moshe's example. He did not say, "Since He who sent me knows the answer to His message, I need not relate it."

19:13 Let no hand touch [the mountain], for he shall be stoned or cast down. Neither man nor beast will be allowed to live. But when the ram's horn is sounded with a long blast, they will then be allowed to climb the mountain.

THE RAM'S HORN—This was the horn of the ram that Avraham sacrificed instead of Yitzchak.

19:16 It came to pass on the third day in the morning, that there were thunder claps and lightning, with a

heavy cloud and an extremely loud blast on the mountain. The people in the camp trembled.

IN THE MORNING—This teaches that He came [to the mountain] before they did. Mortal man does not act in this fashion, with a teacher waiting for his student. Similarly we find [that G-d waited for Yechezkel.] G-d told Yechezkel, *Arise! Go out to the valley.* [Yechezkel then said,] *Thereupon I rose and went out to the valley, and behold, the glory of Hashem was [already] standing there* (*Yechezkel* 3:22, 23).

19:17 Moshe led the people out of the camp to greet G-d. They stood at the foot of the mountain.

TO GREET G-D—The *Shechinah* went out to greet them, like a groom goes out to greet his bride. Therefore the verse says, *Hashem came from Sinai,* not, *Hashem came to Sinai.*

AT THE FOOT OF THE MOUNTAIN—The plain meaning is "at the foot of the mountain." However the Midrash explains that the literal translation is "beneath the mountain" teaching that the mountain was uprooted from its place and suspended over them like a barrel. [G-d said, "If you accept the Torah, fine. If not, this will be your grave."]

19:18 Mount Sinai was completely covered in smoke, because Hashem had come down on it in fire. Its smoke went up like the smoke of a furnace, and the entire mountain trembled violently.

A FURNACE—You may think [Mount Sinai smoked] like a furnace, but not more [than a furnace]. To teach otherwise, the verse says, *The mountain was burning with fire that reached the heart of heaven* (*Devarim* 4:11). Why does the Torah compare [the smoke at Mount Sinai] to that of a furnace? It used an analogy that the human ear can understand. [The Torah] speaks in terms that people can comprehend. Similarly, it says about G-d, *He will roar like a lion* (*Hoshea* 10:11). Who but G-d gave the lion power to roar? Yet Scripture compares G-d to a lion. He is compared to His creatures, using metaphors we can understand. The same is true for the verse, *His voice was like the sound of many waters* (*Yechezkel* 43:2). Who but He gave sound to the waters? Yet G-d's power is compared to the power of His creatures to enable people to comprehend.

19:19 **There was the sound of the ram's horn growing increasingly stronger. Moshe spoke and G-d replied with a Voice.**

GROWING INCREASINGLY STRONGER—When mortals blow [a shofar,] the longer one blows, the weaker and more faint the sound becomes; yet here it grew increasingly stronger. Why was it [weaker at first]? In order to accustom their ears to the sound, [and not shock them with a startling phenomenon].

19:21 **Hashem said to Moshe: "Go back down and warn the people lest they cross the boundary to see Hashem, and many will die."**

AND MANY WILL DIE—Even if a single individual falls, I will consider it as if many had fallen.

19:24 **Hashem said to him, "Go down. You can then come back up along with Aharon. But the kohanim and the people must not violate the boundary to go up to Hashem, lest He send destruction among them."**

GO DOWN—And warn them a second time [not to cross the boundary around the mountain.] A person should be urged before the time of action, and then warned again at the moment of action.

THE TEN COMMANDMENTS

20:2 I am Hashem your G-d, who brought you out of Egypt, from the place of slavery.

WHO BROUGHT YOU OUT OF EGYPT—[G-d identified Himself through the Exodus rather than as the Creator of the universe declaring that] the fact that I took you out of Egypt is sufficient [reason] for you to serve Me.

Another explanation [why G-d associated Himself with the Exodus is,] because He revealed Himself at the [parting of the sea] as a valiant warrior, and here [at Sinai] He revealed Himself as an elderly compassionate man, as it says, *They saw a vision of the G-d of Yisrael, and under is feet was something like a sapphire brick, and something like the essence of a clear blue sky* (*Shemos* 24:10). The brick was before Him [to remind Him of the Jews who were forced to make bricks] during the enslavement. However once they were redeemed [G-d rejoiced and the brick was replaced with] *something like the essence of a clear blue sky.* [Said G-d,] "Do not think that since I change appearances, there are two divine powers, for I am the One who brought you out of Egypt, and I am the One who performed the miracles at the [parting of] the sea."

Another reason [G-d mentioned the Exodus was because] they heard many sounds [at the time of the revelation at Sinai], as it says, *All the people saw the sounds* (ibid. 20:15). Since the sounds came from the four directions and from heaven and earth, they may have thought there are many divine powers. To teach otherwise [Hashem said, I am the same one who took you out at the Exodus where it was obvious that I was alone.]

20:6 I show loving-kindness for thousands of generations for those who love Me and keep My commandments.

I SHOW LOVING-KINDNESS FOR THOUSANDS OF GENERATIONS— [G-d] safeguards the kindness a person does and rewards his descendants for two thousand generations. It follows that [G-d's] measure of bestowing reward is five hundred times greater than His measure of punishment, for [His punishment] lasts only four generations, (ibid.20:4) whereas His reward lasts two thousand generations.

20:9 **You shall work during the six weekdays and all your work shall be done.**

AND ALL YOUR WORK SHALL BE DONE—When Shabbos comes, consider it as if all your work were done and do not even think about work.

20:11 **It was during the six weekdays that Hashem made the heaven, the earth, and all that is in them, and He rested on the seventh day. Hashem therefore blessed the Shabbos day and made it holy.**

AND HE RESTED ON THE SEVENTH DAY—[G-d] wrote about Himself that He rested, as if it were possible [for G-d to become tired]. [He wrote this so people would] draw a logical conclusion from Him. [If G-d, who created everything with His word, rested on Shabbos,] how much more so, man, whose labor is done through toil and exertion, should rest on Shabbos.

BLESSED THE SHABBOS DAY AND MADE IT HOLY—*He blessed it* with the manna, giving double the usual amount on Friday as a, "double bread." *He made it holy* with the manna, since it did not come down on Shabbos.

20:15 **All the people saw the sounds, the lightning, the sound of the shofar, and the mountain smoking. The people trembled when they saw it and kept their distance.**

ALL THE PEOPLE SAW—This teaches us that not a single blind person was among them. And from where do we know there was no mute among them? Because it says, *All the people answered* (*Shemos*

19:8). And from where do we know there was no deaf person among them? Because it says, *We will do and we will listen* (ibid. 5:6).

SAW THE SOUNDS—They saw things that can only be heard, which is impossible to see anywhere else.

20:17 "Do not be afraid," Moshe replied to the people. "G-d came in order to raise you up, and in order that His fear will be on your faces, so that you will not sin."

TO RAISE YOU UP—To elevate you in the [eyes of the] world, so your reputation can spread among the nations, [who will recognize] that He in His glory revealed Himself to you.

HIS FEAR WILL BE ON YOUR FACES—Because you saw Him as fearsome and dreaded, you will know there is none beside Him, and you will therefore be in awe of Him.

20:22 When you will eventually build a stone altar for Me, do not build it of out of cut stone, lest you lift your sword against it [to cut the stones], and you will have profaned it.

AND YOU WILL HAVE PROFANED IT—You can conclude from this that lifting iron over it will profane it, because the altar was created to lengthen man's life, and iron [which is used to make swords] was created to shorten man's life; it is not right that the device used to shorten life be lifted over the means of lengthening life. Furthermore, since the altar makes peace between Yisrael and their Father in Heaven, nothing that cuts and destroys should come over it. This leads to a logical conclusion: If the Torah says, *Do not lift iron,* over stones which neither see, hear nor speak, because they make peace, surely no harm will come to one who makes peace between man and his wife, between one family and another, and between one man and another.

20:23
Do not climb up to My altar with steps, so that your nakedness not be revealed on it.

SO THAT YOUR NAKEDNESS NOT BE REVEALED ON IT—because such steps force one to take wide strides. Although [the steps] did not actually cause nakedness to be exposed, for [the *kohanim* wore pants,] as it says, *Make for them linen pants* (*Shemos* 28:42), nevertheless, taking wide steps is akin to exposing nakedness, and thus demeans the stones of the altar. These matters give rise to a logical conclusion: If the Torah says, "Though the stones do not sense humiliation, since they fill a need, do not treat them a disdainful manner," how much more so [must one be careful not to humiliate] his fellow man who is created in the image of His Creator and is grieved by his humiliation.

מ ש פ ט י ם
MISHPATIM

—◦◉◦—

21:1 These are the laws that you must set before them.

THAT YOU MUST SET BEFORE THEM—[Why doesn't it say, "That you must teach them"?]—The Holy One, blessed be He, said to Moshe, "Don't let it enter your mind to say, 'I will teach them the chapter [of the Written Torah] or the law [of the Oral Torah] two or three times, until they can recite it the way I taught them. I will not trouble to make them understand the reasons and explanation of the subject matter.'" Therefore it says, *that you must set before them*, [so that it is easily understood,] like a set table with everything ready to be eaten.

BEFORE THEM—But not before non-Jewish [judges]. Even if you know [the non-Jewish judges] will decide a case according to the laws of Yisrael, do not bring it to their courts, because bringing Jewish lawsuits before a non-Jewish court desecrates the name of G-d and honors the name of deities, conferring [undue] importance on them, as it says, *For their rock* [their god] *is not like our Rock* [our G-d], *and yet our enemies judge us* (*Devarim* 32:11). Letting our enemies judge us, testifies to [our] esteem of their deities.

21:6

His master[19] will bring him [the slave] to the courts. Bringing him near the door or the doorpost, his master shall pierce his ear with an awl.

HIS MASTER SHALL PIERCE HIS EAR—Why was the ear rather than any other part of the body chosen to be pierced? Rabban Yochanan ben Zakkai said: His ear heard at Mount Sinai, *Do not steal* (*Shemos* 20:13), yet he stole, so let it be pierced. And if [he did not steal but] sold himself [as a slave willingly,] his ear heard at Mount Sinai, *The children of Yisrael are to be [exclusively] My slaves* (*Vayikra* 25:55), yet he acquired a [different] master for himself, so let it be pierced.

Rabbi Shimon expounded this verse [as pleasingly] as a pouch of fragrant spices, stating: Why were the door and doorpost singled out from all other parts of the house? The Holy One, blessed be He, said, "The door and doorpost were witnesses in Egypt [on the night of Pesach] that I passed over the lintel and two doorposts, saying, *The children of Yisrael are slaves unto Me.* I implied, "They are My slaves, and not slaves of slaves," yet this person [by extending his term of servitude] acquired a [different] master for himself, let his ear be pierced publicly.

21:13

If he did not plan to kill [his victim][20], but G-d caused it to happen, then I will provide a place where [the killer] can find refuge.

BUT G-D CAUSED IT TO HAPPEN—Why would G-d allow such a thing to happen? David [answered this question in the verse], *As the ancient proverb says: Evil comes forth from evil ones* (1 *Shemuel* 24:14). The ancient proverb refers to the Torah, the proverb of the Holy One, blessed be He, who is the Ancient One of the universe. Where does the Torah say, *Evil comes forth from evil ones?* In our

---

[19] A Jewish slave wishing to remain with his master after his term of enslavement, pierces his ear and remains a permanent slave.
[20] One who kills unintentionally must be exiled.

verse, *But G-d caused it to happen,* which is about two people who killed, one accidentally and the other intentionally. Since there were no witnesses, the one who killed intentionally was not executed, nor was the one who killed accidentally exiled. The Holy One, blessed be He, orchestrates events so eventually they both lodge at the same inn. The one who killed intentionally sits beneath a ladder, while the one who killed accidentally climbs the ladder and falls on the former, killing him. Witnesses testify [about the incident,] making the latter liable to exile. Thus the one who had killed accidentally is exiled, and the one who killed intentionally is killed.

21:37 If a person steals an ox or a sheep and then slaughters or sells it, he must repay five cattle for each ox and four sheep for each sheep.

FIVE CATTLE FOR EACH OX—Rabbi Yochanan ben Zakkai said: The Omnipresent is careful with a person's dignity. Since an ox walks on his own legs, the thief is not humiliated by carrying it on his shoulders, so he must pay five oxen. However, [the thief] must carry a sheep on his shoulders; because he was embarrassed by [carrying] it, he pays only four sheep.

Rabbi Meir said: Come and see how great work is considered. For the ox which [pulls the plow, and] was prevented from working, he must pay five oxen, but for stealing a sheep which does not work, he pays only four sheep.

22:20 Do not hurt the feelings of a foreigner or oppress him, for you were foreigners in Egypt.

FOR YOU WERE FOREIGNERS IN EGYPT—If you hurt his feelings, he can hurt your feelings likewise, by saying to you, "You too, descend from strangers." Do not taunt another, with a fault you have yourself.

22:24 When you lend money to My people, to the poor man who is together with you, do not press him for repayment. Do not take interest from him.

TO MY PEOPLE—Do not act disdainfully when lending someone money, for he is of My people.

TO THE POOR MAN WHO IS TOGETHER WITH YOU—[Put yourself in his shoes,] as if you also considered yourself poor.

22:30 Be My holy people. Do not eat flesh torn off in the field [by a predator.] Cast it to the dogs.

BE MY HOLY PEOPLE—If you sanctify yourselves by abstaining [from eating] loathsome *neveilos* and *tereifos* [animals that were not slaughtered and animals that suffered lethal injury], then you are Mine. But if not, you are not Mine.

CAST IT TO THE DOGS—[This is not meant literally,] for it can be sold to a non-Jew. Or perhaps [you may not sell the meat to a non-Jew,] and the phrase, *to the dogs* is meant literally? To teach you otherwise, the Torah says, *you may sell it to a non-Jew (Devarim 14:21)* regarding *neveilah*[21]. [If one may derive benefit from an animal that died without being slaughtered,] surely one is permitted to derive benefit from a *tereifah*[22]. If so, why did the Torah say, *cast it to the dogs?* To teach you that G-d does not withhold the reward due to any creature. [At the exodus from Egypt it says, *But among all the children of Yisrael, a dog will not bark (Shemos 11:7)*, therefore, the Holy One, blessed be He, said, "Give [the dog] its reward [by casting your meat to it.]"

23:7 Keep away from anything false. Do not kill a person who is innocent or one who is righteous, for I will not let a guilty person escape punishment.

FOR I WILL NOT LET A GUILTY PERSON ESCAPE PUNISHMENT—It is not your duty to remand [a defendant who has been acquitted,

---

[21] An animal that died without being slaughtered.
[22] Aan animal that suffered a lethal injury by selling it to a non-Jew.

even if new evidence of his guilt is presented,] for I will not acquit him when I judge him. Though he emerges innocent from your court, I have many agents to put him to death as he deserves.

23:8 Do not accept bribery, because bribery blinds the clear-sighted and twists the words of the just.

BRIBERY BLINDS THE CLEAR-SIGHTED—Despite being a Torah scholar, if he takes a bribe, he will become [morally] confused, forgetting his learning, and causing his eyesight to grow dim.

23:20 I will send an angel before you[23] to safeguard you on the way, and to bring you to the place that I have prepared.

TO THE PLACE THAT I HAVE PREPARED—The simple interpretation of this verse is: [To the Beis Hamikdash,] which I have prepared for you [in the future]. According to the Midrash the verse should be interpreted as follows: *To the place that I have [already] established.* [For the heavenly Beis Hamikdash] already exists opposite [the Beis Hamikdash which will be built on earth]. This is one of the verses [in Tanach] indicating that the heavenly Beis Hamikdash is directly in line with the earthly Beis Hamikdash.

24:10 They saw [a vision] of the G-d of Yisrael[24], and under His feet there was something like a sapphire brick and like the essence of a clear blue sky.

THEY SAW [A VISION] OF THE G-D OF YISRAEL—They intentionally gazed and perceived, and therefore deserved to die. Because the Holy One, blessed be He, did not want to spoil the joy of [the receiving of] the Torah, He waited until the day of the inauguration

---

[23] After the sin of the golden calf, Hashem offered to send an angel to lead the Jewish people into Eretz Yisrael and the Beis Hamikdash.

[24] At the giving of the Torah, Nadad, Avihu and the Elders gazed at G-d.

of the Mishkan [to carry out the death sentence] of Nadav and Avihu, and [He waited] until [the incident referred to in the verse,] *The people began to complain . . . and G-d's fire flared out consuming the edge of the camp (Bamidbar* 11:1), [to carry out the death sentence] of the elders. The phrase *the edge of the camp*, [is interpreted as] "among the leaders of the camp," meaning, the elders.

SOMETHING LIKE A SAPPHIRE BRICK—[The brick] stayed in front of Him during the time of [Yisrael's] slavery, as a reminder of the agony of Yisrael who were enslaved [and forced] to make bricks.

LIKE THE ESSENCE OF A CLEAR BLUE SKY—[To symbolize that] once they were redeemed there was light and joy before Him.

24:12 Hashem said to Moshe: "Come up to Me to the mountain and remain there. I will give to you the stone tablets, the Torah and the commandments that I have written [for the people's] instruction."

THE STONE TABLETS, THE TORAH AND THE COMMANDMENTS THAT I HAVE WRITTEN [FOR THE PEOPLE'S] INSTRUCTION—All 613 commandments are contained in the Ten Commandments. Rabbeinu Saadiah Gaon[25] composed the *Azharos*, showing how each of the 613 mitzvos relates to one of the Ten Commandments.

---

25 Rabbeinu Saadiah Gaon (582-942 c.e.), was the greatest scholar of the Gaonic period. As head of the yeshivah in Pumbedisa, he was the leader of world Jewry. His *Emunos Vedeyos* is considered one of the most important works on Jewish philosophy.

תרומה
TERUMAH

———═◆═———

BUILDING THE MISHKAN

25:5 [They donated to the Mishkan,] Reddened rams' skins, tachash skins, and *shittim* [acacia] wood.

AND ACACIA WOOD—Where did they find *shittim* wood in the desert? Rabbi Tanchuma explains that our forefather Yaakov foreseeing with divine inspiration that the Jews would build a *Mishkan* in the wilderness, brought *shittim* trees to Egypt, planting them there. He instructed his sons to take them along when they left Egypt.

25:16 It is in this ark that you will place the testimony that I will give you.

THE TESTIMONY—Refers to the Torah, which is a testimony between Me and you that I commanded you the mitzvos that are written in it.

26:15 Make the [upright] beams for the Mishkan out of *shittim* wood.

MAKE THE [UPRIGHT] BEAMS—It should have said: "Make [upright] beams," as is said [in the description of] each of the other

94

furnishings of the Mishkan. Why does it add [the word *the* in] *Make the upright beams*? They are to take the beams which have already been set aside for this purpose. Our father Yaakov planted *shittim* trees in Egypt, commanding his sons on his deathbed to take them along when they left Egypt, explaining that the Holy One, blessed be He, would command them in the future to make a Mishkan of *shittim* wood in the wilderness, and they must have the wood on hand, ready [to be installed]. This is what the Babylonian [composer wrote in his *piyut* for the first day of Pesach:]26 "[The trees Yaakov] planted for his diligent [sons] were hastily brought [to the wilderness] to become the cedar beams of our House [the Mishkan]." They are called diligent sons because they diligently made sure that [the beams] were on hand and ready before [the command to build the Mishkan].

---

26 From the *piyut* beginning with the words *Ohr yesha*, in the lines beginning with the letter *tes*.

———❦———

28:12 Place the two stones on the two shoulder pieces of the apron[27] as remembrance stones for the children of Yisrael. Aharon shall carry their names on his two shoulders before Hashem as a remembrance.

AS A REMEMBRANCE—The Holy One, blessed be He, will see the names of the tribes written before Him and remember their righteousness.

29:18 Burn the entire ram on the altar; it is a burnt-offering to Hashem. It shall thus be a satisfying fragrance, a fire-offering to Hashem.

A SATISFYING FRAGRANCE—My satisfaction is derived from commanding, and having My will obeyed.

29:36 Sacrifice a young bull as a sin offering each day for the cleansings. By sprinkling [the blood of this of-

---

[27] One of the vestments of the High Priest was an apron with two stones inscribed with the names of the Tribes of Yisrael on the shoulder straps.

fering] on the altar you will atone for [any misdeed associated with making] it, and by anointing it you will sanctify it.

FOR THE CLEANSINGS—The *Midrash Toras Kohanim* says that it was necessary to atone on the altar because someone may have stolen an article and donated it for the work of the Mishkan and the altar.

30:16 You will take this atonement money from the children of Yisrael and use it for making the Tent of Meeting. It will thus be a remembrance for the children of Yisrael before Hashem to atone for your souls.

USE IT FOR MAKING THE TENT OF MEETING—We learn from this, that [Moshe] was commanded to count [the children of Yisrael] when they began contributing toward the Mishkan after the episode of the golden calf. [The command was given at that time] because a plague had struck them, as it says, *Hashem struck the people with a plague* (*Shemos* 32:35). This can be compared to a flock of valuable sheep that was stricken with a plague. Once [the disease] ended, the owner told the shepherd, "Please count my sheep to find out how many are left." [So too, Hashem] is indicating how precious we are to him.

30:31 Speak to the children of Yisrael and tell them, "This shall be the sacred anointing oil to Me for all generations."

FOR ALL GENERATIONS—Our Rabbis inferred from here that all [the anointing oil made by Moshe] still exists. [It will be used for anointing] in time to come [when Moshiach comes and the Beis Hamikdash is rebuilt].

30:34 Hashem said to Moshe: "Take [the following] spices: balsam, onycha, galbanum, spices and pure frankincense, all of the same weight."

GALBANUM—This spice has an offensive odor. The Torah includes it among the components of the incense to teach us not to look askance at sinners of Yisrael. Rather they should be included in our gatherings for fasts and prayers.

31:13 And you speak to the children of Israel and say to them: "You must keep My Shabbos. For it is a sign between Me and you for all generations, to make known that I, Hashem, am making you holy."

FOR IT IS A SIGN BETWEEN ME AND YOU—This great sign attests to our relationship. Granting My day of rest for [your] rest, [shows] that I have chosen you.

TO MAKE KNOWN—The nations will know through [the Shabbos] that it is I, Hashem, who makes you holy.

31:17 It is an everlasting sign between Me and the children of Yisrael that during the six weekdays Hashem made heaven and earth, but on the seventh day He ceased working and He rested.

AND HE RESTED—[The Hebrew for "And He rested" is, *Vayinafash*.] The word *nofesh*, "relaxation" [which is the root of *vayinafash*] is related to *nefesh*, "soul or spirit," for one's spirit is refreshed when he relaxes from the toil of work.

[G-d,] about whom it says, *He never grows faint or weary* (*Yeshayah* 40:23), and all of His works are performed through mere speech, applied the term "rest" to Himself, so the human mind could grasp [this concept].

31:18 When He [Hashem] finished speaking with him on Mount Sinai, He gave him two tablets of the Testimony. They were stone tablets, written with the finger of G-d.

WHEN HE [HASHEM] FINISHED—[The Hebrew for "When He finished" is, *Kechaloso*.] The word *kechaloso* is written in abbreviated form [the *vav* between the *lamed* and the *tav* is missing], and can also be read as *kekalaso*, "like his bride." The Torah was handed to Moshe as a gift, the way a bride is given to a groom; otherwise he could not have learned it in such a short time.

Another explanation: Just as a bride is adorned with twenty-four ornaments—listed in the Book of Yeshayah (3:18-22)—so too, a Torah scholar must be adorned [and well-versed] with the twenty-four books [of Tanach].

SPEAKING WITH HIM—This teaches us that Moshe heard [the law] from G-d, and then they reviewed the law together.

THE SIN OF THE GOLDEN CALF

32:5 Aharon saw and he built an altar before [the calf]. Aharon made an announcement saying: "Tomorrow, there will be a festival to Hashem."

TOMORROW, THERE WILL BE A FESTIVAL TO HASHEM—[Aharon did not say,] "today," [hoping] that Moshe would return before they worshiped [the golden calf]. This is the plain meaning of the text.

The Midrashic interpretation to this verse is found in *Vayikra Rabbah* 10:3. Aharon [built the altar because he] saw many things. He saw Chur, the son of his sister [Miriam], killed by the people after he admonished them. Accordingly, the passage, [*Va'yiven mizbei'ach lefanav*]—*He built an altar before [the calf]*, should be read as, *va'yaven mizavu'ach lefanav—from the slaughtered body [lying] before him he realized.*

He also saw [the outrage] and said, "Better that I be blamed [for this sin] than they."

He saw yet another thing and said, "If they build the altar, one will bring a pebble and the other will bring a stone, and as a result, the work will be completed at once. But if I alone build it, I can stall the work, and in the meantime Moshe will come."

A FESTIVAL TO HASHEM—He made [his announcement] with his heart for the sake of G-d, hoping that Moshe would arrive, and the people would worship G-d.

32:6 Getting up early the next morning, [the people] sacrificed burnt offerings and brought peace offerings. The people sat down to eat and drink, and they got up to behave promiscuously.

THEY GOT UP TO BEHAVE PROMISCUOUSLY—the [seemingly superfluous] phrase, *they got up* implies that Satan roused them to make them sin.

32:7 Hashem said to Moshe: "Go down, for your people you brought out of Egypt have become corrupt."

GO DOWN—[Meaning:] "Go down from your exalted stature. I gave you this high position only for their sake." At that moment Moshe was banished by the heavenly Court.

YOUR PEOPLE HAVE BECOME CORRUPT—It does not say, "the people," but rather, "your people have become corrupt," implying: It is the rabble [of non-Jews] you accepted on your own initiative, converting them without consulting Me, declaring, "It is a good thing for converts to be brought close to the *Shechinah*"—that became corrupt and corrupted others."

32:10
Now, do not try to stop Me[28], when I unleash My wrath against them to destroy them; I will then make you into a great nation.

DO NOT TRY TO STOP ME—Although Moshe had not yet prayed for Yisrael, G-d said, *"Do not try to stop Me."* He thereby gave [Moshe] an opening, indicating that the matter depends on him; if he prayed for them, G-d would not destroy them.

MOSHE PRAYS FOR THE BNEI YISRAEL

32:13
Remember Your servants, Avraham, Yitzchak, and Yisrael. You swore to them by Your Self, declaring, "I shall increase your descendants as numerous as the stars of the sky, and the entire land of which I spoke I shall give to your descendants, so that they will be able to occupy it forever."

REMEMBER AVRAHAM—If they transgressed the Ten Commandments, [remember that] their forefather Avraham was tested through ten trials and has not yet received his reward. Give it to him now, so "the ten" will cancel "the ten."

AVRAHAM, YITZCHAK, AND YISRAEL—If [Yisrael is to be punished] by burning, *remember Avraham* who offered himself to be burned for Your sake in Ur Kasdim. If [they are condemned to be killed] by the sword, remember Yitzchak who stretched forth his neck [to be slaughtered] at the *Akeidah* [the Binding of Yitzchak]. If [they are to be punished] by exile, remember Yaakov who went into exile to Charan. And if [Yisrael] cannot be saved by the merit of their forefathers, then why are You telling me, *I will then make you into a great nation*? If a chair with three legs cannot stand before You

---

28 Hashem asked that Moshe not stop Him from punishing the Jewish people.

when You are angry, much less will a chair with one leg be able to stand.

YOU SWORE TO THEM BY YOUR SELF—You did not swear to them by something that has an end—such as the heavens, the earth, the mountains, and the hills. Rather, [You swore] by Your Own Self, for You endure forever, and Your oath endures forever, as it was said, [to Avraham], *I have sworn by My Own Self, says Hashem* (*Bereishis* 22:16), and as it was said to Yitzchak, *I will keep the oath that I made to your Father Avraham* (ibid. 26:3), and as it was said to Yaakov, *I am E-l Shad-dai. Be fruitful and increase* (ibid. 35:41). He swore to [Yaakov] by [the Name] *E-l Shad-dai* [which denotes His Own Self].

32:15 Moshe turned around and went down the mountain with the two Tablets of Testimony in his hand. They were tablets written on both sides, with the writing visible from either side.

ON BOTH SIDES—Miraculously the letters could be read [from both sides of the tablets].

32:16 The Tablets were the work of G-d, and the script was G-d's script, engraved on the Tablets.

THE TABLETS WERE THE WORK OF G-D—Its plain meaning is that G-d in His glory made them Himself.

Another explanation: [This should be translated as, *The tablets are the occupation of G-d,*] like one who tells his friend, "So-and-so is totally occupied in his profession." Here too, the Holy One, blessed be He, only finds delight in the study of Torah.

32:19 As he approached the camp, he saw the calf and the dancing. Moshe's anger was aroused and he threw down the Tablets that were in his hands, shattering them at the foot of the mountain.

HE THREW DOWN THE TABLETS THAT WERE IN HIS HANDS—He reasoned: The Torah says, *No apostate may eat of it* (*Shemos* 12:43), regarding the *Pesach* offering which is [only] one of the commandments. How can I possibly give [the Ten Commandments, which comprise all 613 mitzvos of] the entire Torah, to Yisrael when they are all apostates?

32:34 Now go, lead the people to [the place] that I described to you. Behold, I will send an angel before you. When I make an accounting, I will take the sin of theirs into account.

WHEN I MAKE AN ACCOUNTING, I WILL TAKE THE SIN OF THEIRS INTO ACCOUNT—Although I have listened to you, desisting from destroying them all at once, whenever I make an accounting of their sins, I will count a portion of this sin along with their other sins. Thus, there is no punishment that comes on Yisrael that does not contain some retribution for the sin of the golden calf.

33:3 [You will thus go] to a land flowing with milk and honey. However, I will not go up with you, since you are a stiff-necked people, and I may destroy you along the way.

SINCE YOU ARE A STIFF-NECKED PEOPLE—Were My *Shechinah* in your midst, when you rebelled against Me, I would have to deal with you with heightened fury.

33:7 Moshe would take [his] tent and set it up outside the camp at a distance. He called it the Meeting Tent. Whoever sought Hashem would go to the Meeting Tent outside the camp.

MOSHE WOULD TAKE HIS TENT—[Since *would take*,] denotes a recurring action, [the verse is to be interpreted:] From the time of the sin and onward, Moshe pitched his tent outside the camp, saying, "One who is banished from his Master [should be] banished from the student." [Since G-d distanced Himself from the people saying, *I will not go up with you* (33:3), Moshe also distanced himself from them, pitching his tent outside the camp].

WHOEVER SOUGHT HASHEM WOULD GO TO THE MEETING TENT— [It should have said, *Whoever sought Moshe.*] From here we learn that one who seeks the presence of a [Torah] sage is likened to one who seeks the presence of the *Shechinah*.

WHOEVER SOUGHT HASHEM WOULD GO TO THE MEETING TENT— Another interpretation: Even when ministering angels searched for Hashem asking, "Where is the place of the *Shechinah?*" their colleagues answered, "Look, He is in Moshe's tent."

33:8 Whenever Moshe went out to the tent, the people would all rise, and each person would stand near his own tent, gazing at Moshe until he came to the tent.

GAZING AT MOSHE—In admiration, [declaring,] "Fortunate is he, a man born of woman, who can be confident that the *Shechinah* will follow him into the entrance of his tent.

33:11 Hashem would speak to Moshe face to face, as a man would speak to his close friend. [Moshe] would then return to the camp, but his aide, the young man Yehoshua son of Nun, did not leave the tent.

[MOSHE] WOULD THEN RETURN TO THE CAMP—Its Midrashic explanation is: *Hashem would speak to Moshe,* telling him to return to the camp, saying, "I am angry [at Yisrael], and you are angry [at Yisrael. If so, who will influence them [to repent]?" [Thereupon Moshe would return to the camp.]

33:16 Unless You accompany us, how will it be known that I and Your people are pleasing to You. [But if You do,] I and Your people will be distinguished from every nation on the face of the earth.

HOW WILL IT BE KNOWN—How will it be known that we are pleasing to You, *unless You accompany us.*

I AND YOUR PEOPLE WILL BE DISTINGUISHED FROM EVERY NATION ON THE FACE OF THE EARTH—I ask yet another thing from You, that You no longer rest Your *Shechinah* on the [other] nations of the world.

33:18 [Moshe] said: "Please let me have a vision of Your glory."

PLEASE LET ME HAVE A VISION OF YOUR GLORY—Because Moshe saw it was a time of [Divine] favor, with his words being accepted, he additionally requested, that G-d show him the vision of His glory.

33:19 [Hashem] replied: "I will make all My goodness pass before you, and call out the Name Hashem in your presence, and I shall show favor when I show favor, and I shall have mercy when I shall have mercy.

I WILL MAKE ALL MY GOODNESS PASS BEFORE YOU—The time has come to show you as much of My glory as I will allow you to see, because I need to teach you the order of prayer. When you pleaded for mercy for Yisrael, you asked Me to remember the merit of the forefathers, thinking that if the merit of the forefathers runs out, there is no longer hope. [To teach you otherwise,] I will let all the Attributes of My goodness pass before you on the rock while you are hidden in a cave.

AND I WILL CALL OUT THE NAME HASHEM BEFORE YOU—Teaching you the method of asking for mercy, even if the merit of the forefathers runs out. Just as you see Me wrapped [in a *tallis*] and proclaiming the Thirteen Attributes, teach Yisrael to do likewise. If they mention [My divine Attributes,] *Merciful and Gracious,* before Me, they will be answered, for My compassion is boundless.

AND I SHOW FAVOR WHEN I SHOW FAVOR—At those times when I want to show favor.

AND I SHALL HAVE MERCY WHEN I SHALL HAVE MERCY—At those times when I want to have mercy. Until this point, He promised [Moshe] that [if they mention the Thirteen Attributes,] "sometimes I will answer their prayers and sometimes I will not answer them." When He actually [revealed the Thirteen Attributes to Moshe], He said, *I will make a covenant* (*Shemos* 34:10), promising [Moshe] that [the Thirteen Attributes invoked in prayer] will never remain unanswered.

33:21 Hashem said: Behold, there is a place with Me, where you can stand on the rock.

BEHOLD, THERE IS A PLACE WITH ME—On the mountain where I always speak to you I have set aside a special place where I will hide you, so you will not be hurt [by seeing My Presence,] and from there you will see what you will see. This is its plain meaning. Its Midrashic interpretation is: The phrase, *[There is a place with Me* does not refer to a place on the mountain, rather it means] "the place" is with the *Shechinah.* For the Holy One, blessed be He, is the place of the world, [and all place exists within Him] but His world is not His place.

34:1 Hashem said to Moshe, "Carve out two tablets for yourself, just like the first ones. I will write on these tablets the same words that were on the first tablets that you broke."

CARVE OUT FOR YOURSELF—"You broke the first ones. You carve out the others yourself." A parable: A king went abroad and left his betrothed with her maidservants. As a result of the indecent behavior of the maidservants, [false] rumors [of infidelity] about [the betrothed] were circulated. Her guardian tore her *kesubah* (marriage contract), saying, "If the king says she should be killed [because of

her alleged infidelity], I will say to him: 'She is not yet your wife.'"
When the king investigated the matter and found that it was only the
maidservants who were guilty of misconduct, he reconciled with [his
betrothed]. Her guardian said to [the king], "Write another *kesubah*
for her, because the first one was torn up." Replied the king: "You
tore it up, you buy another sheet of paper, and I will personally write
her another *kesubah*." Similarly, the king [in the parable] represents
the Holy One, blessed be He. The maidservants represent the rabble [of non-Jews, Moshe converted, who made the golden calf]. The
guardian is Moshe, and the betrothed of the Holy One, blessed be
He, is Yisrael. Thus it says, *Carve out for yourself.*

34:3 No man may go up with you, and no one else may appear on the entire mountain. Even the cattle and sheep may not graze near the mountain.

NO MAN MAY GO UP WITH YOU—Since the first [Tablets] were given
with tumultuous noise and before a multitude, the evil eye affect-
ed them. [The lesson learned is:] There is nothing better than
modesty.

34:6 Hashem passed by before [Moshe] and proclaimed: "Hashem, Hashem, G-d, Merciful and Gracious, Slow to Anger, and Abundant in Kindness and Truth."

HASHEM, HASHEM—This is an Attribute of Mercy. The first Name
refers to G-d's mercy before a person sins, and the second Name,
refers to His mercy after [a person] sins and repents.

G-D [KEIL]—This, too, is an Attribute of Mercy. [Proof of this can
be found in the verse,] *My G-d! My G-d!* [Keili! Keili!] *Why have
You forsaken me?"* (*Tehillim* 22:2). [If the Name *Keil* referred to
the Attribute of Strict Justice,] it would not make sense to say, *Why
have You forsaken me?* [On the contrary, one would wish to be forsaken by the Attribute of Justice, preferring to be judged by the
Attribute of Mercy.] This I found in *Mechilta.*

SLOW TO ANGER—[means:] It takes a long time until He becomes angry, not hurrying to punish [the sinner], hoping that he will do *teshuvah*.

ABUNDANT IN KINDNESS—For those who need kindness, because they are lacking in merits.

AND TRUTH—To pay a good reward to those who do His will.

34:7 He remembers deeds of kindness for thousands [of generations], forgiving sin, rebellion, and error. He clears, but does not clear [sin] completely, keeping in mind the sins of the fathers on their children and grandchildren, to the third and fourth generation.

HE REMEMBERS DEEDS OF KINDNESS—[To pay the reward for the kindness] that a person does before Him.

FOR THOUSANDS [OF GENERATIONS]—For two thousand generations.

HE CLEARS, BUT DOES NOT CLEAR— According to its simple explanation, *clears and does not clear* means, He does not completely overlook the sin, rather He punishes [the sinner] little by little [so he is able to bear the punishment]. However, our Rabbis interpreted it to mean, He clears those who do *teshuvah* [completely], but does not clear those who do not do *teshuvah*.

KEEPING IN MIND THE SINS OF THE FATHERS ON THEIR CHILDREN AND GRANDCHILDREN—If they carry on the sinful ways of their parents, as it says in another passage, *Where My enemies are concerned, I keep in mind the sin of the fathers for their descendants* (*Shemos* 20:5).

TO THE FOURTH GENERATION—Thus, G-d's measure of good [reward] is five hundred times greater than G-d's measure of punishment. For regarding the measure of good, it says, *He remembers deeds of love for two thousand [generations].*

34:9 He said, "If indeed I find favor in your eyes, my L-rd, let my L-rd go among us, for although this nation is unbending, forgive our sins and errors, and make us Your possession."

AND MAKE US YOUR POSSESSION—Make us Your special possession is the same request as the one mentioned above, *So that I and Your people will be distinguished from every nation on the face of the earth* (*Shemos* 33:16): Do not rest Your *Shechinah* on the nations of the world.

34:10 Hashem said, "Behold, I will make a covenant. Before all Your people I will make wonders the like of which have never been brought into existence in the entire world, among any nation. All the people among whom you dwell will see how fearsome are the deeds that I, Hashem, am doing with you.

I WILL MAKE WONDERS—The word *nifla'os*—"wonders"—is related to the word *veniflinu*—"we will be distinguished" (34:9). You will be distinguished in this respect from all the nations of the world because I will not rest My *Shechinah* on them.

34:29 Moshe came down from Mount Sinai, with the two Tablets of the Testimony in his hands as he descended from the mountain. Moshe did not realize that the skin of his face had become luminous when [Hashem] had spoken to him.

THAT THE SKIN OF HIS FACE HAD BECOME LUMINOUS—The word *karan*—had become luminous—is related to *keren*—horn, for the rays of light radiate, shooting out like a horn. From where did Moshe merit these rays of splendor? Our Rabbis said: From the cave, when the Holy One, Blessed be He, placed His hand on [Moshe's] face, as it says, *I will cover you with My hand* (33:22).

34:30 When Aharon and all Yisrael saw the skin of Moshe's face shining with a brilliant light, they were afraid to come close to him.

THEY WERE AFRAID TO COME CLOSE TO HIM—See how potent is the power of sin. Before they stretched out their hands to sin [with the golden calf], what does it say? *To the children of Yisrael, the appearance of Hashem's glory on the mountain top was like a devouring flame* (24:17), and they were not afraid, nor did they tremble. But once they made the golden calf, they cringed and trembled even from Moshe's rays of splendor.

34:32 After that, all the children of Yisrael approached, and Moshe gave them instructions regarding all that Hashem had told him on Mount Sinai.

AFTER THAT, ALL THE CHILDREN OF YISRAEL APPROACHED—After [Moshe] taught the elders, he repeated the section or halachah to Yisrael. Our Rabbis explain: How was the Torah taught? Moshe learned from the mouth of the Al-mighty. Aharon entered, and Moshe taught him the chapter. Aharon moved over to sit at Moshe's left, and his sons [Elazar and Isamar] entered, and Moshe taught them the chapter. They moved over, Elazar sitting at Moshe's right, and Isamar sitting at Aharon's left. [Then] the elders entered, and Moshe taught them the chapter. The elders moved away and sat on the sides. [Then] the entire nation entered, and Moshe taught them the chapter. Thus, all the people had one [lesson in the chapter], the elders had two, the sons of Aharon had three, Aharon had four . . . as it says in *Eiruvin* 54b.

=====•())•=====

35:27 The princes brought the shoham stones and the filling stones for the *eifod* and the breastplate.

THE PRINCES BROUGHT—Rabbi Nassan said: What prompted the princes to donate to the dedication of the altar [before the rest of the people], whereas they were not the first to donate at the construction of the Mishkan? [At the construction of the Mishkan] the princes said, "Let the people donate whatever they donate, and we will supply the shortfall." The people brought everything, as it says, *All the materials were more than enough* (*Shemos* 37:7). The princes then said, "What is there left for us to do?" They [were only able to] bring the *shoham* stones. Therefore they were the first to donate for the dedication of the Altar. Since they were lazy at first, [not donating right away], a letter was taken from their name, and the word *vehanesi'im* is written defectively [with the *yud* between the *alef* and the *mem* missing].

35:34 [Hashem] also gave to him[28], and Oholiav son of Achisamach, of the tribe of Dan, the ability to teach [others].

---

28 Betzalel, the master craftsman of the Mishkan.

AND OHOLIAV—of the tribe of Dan. Although he was from the sons of one of the maidservants, a low ranking tribe, for the work of the Mishkan the Omnipresent placed him on level with Betzalel, who was from [Yehudah] the greatest of the tribes, to fulfill the verse, *The nobleman is not recognized ahead of the pauper* (*Iyov* 34:19).

38:1 Betzalel made the ark from acacia wood. It was two and a half cubits long, and two and a half cubits wide, and one and a half cubits high.

BETZALEL MADE—Because he devoted himself to the work more than the other wise men, it is called by his name.

38:8 He made the copper washstand and its copper base out of the mirrors of the dedicated women who congregated at the entrance of the Tent of Meeting.

WITH THE MIRRORS OF THE DEDICATED WOMEN WHO CONGRE-GATED—The daughters of Yisrael owned copper mirrors which they looked into when they beautified themselves. They did not keep them for themselves, contributing even these mirrors toward the Mishkan. Since they were intended for sensual purposes, Moshe rejected [the mirrors]. The Holy One, blessed be He, told [Moshe], "Accept them, because I cherish them more than anything else. Through these [mirrors] the women established many legions [of children] in Egypt." When their husbands were exhausted from back-breaking labor, [the women] brought them food and drink, feeding them. Then [the women] took the mirrors, and each one, beholding herself with her husband in the mirror enticed him with words, saying, "I am more beautiful than you." In this way they aroused their husbands' desire to relations. They conceived and gave birth there, as it says, *Under the apple tree I aroused you*" (*Shir Hashirim* 8:5). This is the underlying meaning of, *with the mirrors of the dedicated women who congregated*. The washstand was made of [these mirrors], because its purpose was to make peace between man and his wife, [for if a woman] was warned by her hus-

band [not to seclude herself with a man], and she nevertheless se-
cluded herself with him, the waters of the washstand [proved her
guilt or innocence.] You can be positive that the washstand was
made from donated mirrors [rather than from copper donated for
the rest of the Mishkan], because it says, *The copper of the offering
was seventy* kikar . . . *and he made with it...* (*Shemos* 38:29-31). The
washstand and its base were not mentioned [among the things
made from the seventy *kikar* of copper], so we can conclude that
the copper of the washstand was not from the copper of the offering [but from the copper of the mirrors]. Thus did Rabbi
Tanchuma expound.

פקודי

PEKUDEI

———◦◉◦———

38:21 These are the accounts of the Mishkan, the Mishkan of Testimony which were calculated by Moshe's order, by the Levi'im, under Isamar, son of Aharon the Kohen.

THE MISHKAN, THE MISHKAN—[The word] *Mishkan* is stated twice, alluding to the Beis Hamikdash which was taken as a collateral in its two destructions for the sins of Yisrael.

THE MISHKAN OF TESTIMONY—Testimony for Yisrael, that the Holy One, blessed be He, overlooked the making of the golden calf, for He rested His *Shechinah* among them [in the Mishkan].

38:22 Betzalel, son of Uri, son of Chur of the tribe of Yehudah did all that Hashem had commanded Moshe.

DID ALL THAT HASHEM HAD COMMANDED MOSHE—It does not say: "All that Moshe had commanded him," but rather, *all that Hashem had commanded Moshe*. This implies: [Betzalel, through his own] logic, understood what was said to Moshe on Sinai, including things that his master [Moshe] did not tell him. For Moshe first commanded Betzalel to make the furnishings, and then [commanded him to make] the Mishkan. Betzalel said to him:

"Common sense dictates that first you make the house, and then you put the furnishings into it." [Moshe] replied, "Thus, [as you said] did I hear from the mouth of the Holy One, blessed be He." Moshe continued, "You must have been in G-d's shadow,[30] for as a matter of fact, this is what the Holy One, blessed be He, commanded me." And that is in fact what Betzalel did. He first made the Mishkan, and then he made the furnishings.

39:33 They brought the Mishkan to Moshe. There was the Tent along with its equipment, its furnishings, its beams, crossbars, pillars, and bases.

THEY BROUGHT THE MISHKAN TO MOSHE—Because they were unable to raise it. Since Moshe didn't do work [on the construction] of the Mishkan, the Holy One, blessed be He, left its raising to him. No man was able to raise it because of the weight of the beams, for it was impossible for a man to have the strength to set them upright. However, Moshe raised it. Moshe said to the Holy One, blessed be He, "How can man possibly raise the Mishkan?" [The Holy One, blessed be He,] replied, "Busy yourself [trying to raise it] with your hand." It appeared as if he was raising it, but in fact it rose upright by itself. This is [implied from], *The Mishkan was erected* (40:17)—it was raised by itself.

39:43 When Moshe saw that all the work had been done exactly as Hashem had ordered, he blessed [all the workers].

MOSHE BLESSED [ALL THE WORKERS]—[He said to them:] "May the *Shechinah* rest on the work of your hands, *May the pleasantness of my L-rd be upon us, and [make] the work of our hands . . .* (*Tehillim* 90:1).

---

30 The name Betzalel means 105

GLOSSARY

AGGADAH pl. *AGGADOS* - Homiletic discourses
AVRAHAM - Abraham
BAMIDBAR - The Book of Numbers
BEIS HAMIKDASH - Holy Temple
BEN - son of
BEREISHIS - The Book of Genesis
B'NEI YISRAEL - Children of Israel
CHAMETZ - Leavened bread
DEVARIM - The Book of Deuteronomy
DIVREI HAYAMIM - The Book of Chronicles
EISAV - Esau
ELIYAHU - Elijah
ELOHIM - God
ERETZ YISRAEL - The Land of Israel
GEMARA - Talmud
GEMATRIA - Numerical value of a word
HALACHAH pl. *HALACHOS* - Law
HASHEM - God
HEVEL - Abel
HOSHEA - The Book of Hosea
IYOV - Job
KAYIN - Cain
KEIL - One of the Names of the Almighty
KOHEIN pl. *KOHANIM* - Priests, descendants of Aaron
KOHELES - Ecclesiastes
KOHEN - Priest, descendant of Aharon

LUCHOS - tablets containing the Ten Commandments
MASHIACH - The Messiah
MATZAH pl. *MATZOHS* - Unleavened bread
MELACHIM - The Book of Kings
MIDRASH - A collection of aggadic works.
MISHKAN - The Tabernacle
MISHLEI - Proverbs
MITZVAH pl. *MITZVOS* - commandment
PESACH - Passover
RIVKAH - Rebecca
SHABBOS - The day of rest - Saturday
SHECHINAH - Divine Presence
SHEMOS - The Book of Exodus
SHEMUEL - The Book of Samuel
SHIR HASHIRIM - Song of Songs
SHLOMOH - Solomon
SHOFAR - Ram's horn blown on Rosh Hashana
TALLIS – Prayer Shawl
TANACH - Scriptures
TEFILLIN - Phylacteries
TEHILLIM - Psalms
TESHUVAH - Repentance
TZADDIK pl. *TZADDIKIM* - Pious Person
TZITZIS – Fringes worn on a four cornered garment
VAYIKRA - The Book of Leviticus
YAAKOV - Jacob
YECHEZKEL - Ezekiel
YEHOSHUA - Joshua
YESHAYAH - Isaiah
YIRMIYAH - Jeremiah
YISRAEL - Israel
YITZCHOCK - Isaac
YONAH - Jonah
YOSEF - Joseph